Success in Beginning Reading and Writing

The Basal Concept of the Future

ADDITIONAL TITLES IN THE SUCCESS IN READING AND WRITING SERIES

Success in Kindergarten Reading and Writing
Anne H. Adams, Mary S. Johnson, Judith Connors

Success in Beginning Reading and Writing
Anne H. Adams

Phonics/Spelling Activity Sheets for use with Success in Beginning Reading and Writing

Success in Reading and Writing, Grade Two
Anne H. Adams and Helen Cappleman

Success in Reading and Writing, Grade Three
Anne H. Adams and Mary Johnson

Success in Reading and Writing, Grade Four
Anne H. Adams, Jean Bernholz, Pat Sumner

Success in Reading and Writing, Grade Five
Anne H. Adams, Jean Bernholz, Pat Sumner

Success in Reading and Writing, Grade 6
Anne H. Adams, Elisabeth L. Bebensee

Success in Beginning Reading and Writing

The Basal Concept of the Future

Anne H. Adams, Ed.D.
Duke University

Good Year Books • Glenview, Illinois

To Dr. Anne Flowers, Chairperson of the Duke University Department of Education, who was the first to recognize the concept indicated in the subtitle of this book.

910-BKC-9089

Library of Congress Cataloging in Publication Data

Adams, Anne H.
   Success in beginning reading and writing.

   Includes index.
   1. Reading (Elementary). 2. English language—
Composition and exercises I. Title.
LB1573.A348   372.4   78–6628
ISBN 0–673–16551–5

Contents

Preface

In 1934, Nila Banton Smith, noted reading authority, wrote that the basal reader "may continue to wield its power for fifteen years or for fifty years, but in time it will march silently out of the classroom and be relegated to dusty attics along with its progenitor, the hornbook."[1]

The purpose of this book is twofold. First, it explains a creative system of teaching beginning reading and writing. Second, it affirms that large numbers of first graders can succeed in reading and writing.

Many of us are aware of reading problems that exist in the country today, but it is not always easy to assess the extent of these problems. Despite the United States' relatively high literacy rate, the U.S. Department of Commerce estimated that as of 1969 nearly 1.5 million Americans over fourteen years of age were illiterate, or 1.0 percent of the population.[2] The scope of the problem goes beyond this, however. It is estimated that up to 30 percent of elementary and secondary students have reading difficulties in school,[3] and these problems can damage their effectiveness as functioning members of society. Findings of the Health, Education and Welfare National Advisory Committee on Learning Problems demonstrate further that students of average or above intelligence with low reading ability may perform adequately in the early grades in nonreading subjects but that later performance is significantly lowered. This report also suggests that 75 percent of juvenile delinquents are severely retarded in reading. This problem is not limited solely to poorly adjusted members of society, however. The American Association of Junior Colleges, for example, estimates that one-third to one-half of their new students have significant reading problems.

---

[1]From *American Reading Instruction* by Nila Banton Smith, copyright 1934 by Silver, Burdett and Company. Reprinted by permission of Silver, Burdett and Company.

[2]U.S. Department of Commerce, Bureau of the Census, *Current Population Reports*, Series P-20, Nos. 45, 99, 112, and 217.

[3]Robert Karlin, *Teaching Elementary Reading: Principles and Strategies*, second ed. (New York: Harcourt Brace Jovanovich, 1975), p. 3.

If one in twenty, or 5 percent, of the 51.5 million people in elementary and secondary schools is retained, the annual taxpayer expense is $1.7 billion.[4] The reading problem thus has not only educational but social and economic implications as well. All of this points to the need for improvements in the teaching of reading during the early school years.

There is a national cry for assurance that children will learn to read and write, preferably by the end of the first grade. Although concern has been voiced for several decades—in the form of vast sums of money, countless writings about the subject, and untold hours of labor—there still is not a calming assurance to the public that the schools can accomplish what most people regard as the basic educational charge: successful teaching of reading and writing.

The production and distribution of materials aimed at the teaching of reading have become one of the largest commercial enterprises within the educational system, while writing materials are somewhat less widely available. Instructional materials designed to help children improve their reading skills have appeared in all kinds of colors and shapes—books, kits, stencils, game boxes, files, tapes, transparencies, and checksheets—to name only a few. Thousands of teaching and learning activities have appeared in manuals, spiral-bound books, file cards, and inservice sheets. Changes have been recommended from one approach to another—using strange alphabet symbols, drilling specific reading skills, dutifully following teachers' editions for basal readers, reciting phonics rules, providing programmed answers, and so on—in efforts to teach children whose abilities and interests were not the same. Throughout it all, the literacy levels and interest in reading seemed to deteriorate rather than improve.

Although I did not realize it at the time, research for this book began in 1964 when I found myself under contract to teach 36 first graders, none of whom could read. It was one of the most frustrating years of my professional life; however, through those experiences I began to identify some of the major problems and concerns expressed orally or in the literature with specific reference to beginning reading instruction.

My approach was direct. I tried to analyze each problem as a springboard for an exploration of alternatives that might eliminate or alleviate the problem. Part of the analysis was my doctoral dissertation, in which I researched the concept of correlated language arts in the first grade without use of basal readers.

Until 1976, the contents of this book were in the form of a rough draft and had become one of those things "I would finish one day soon." Matters were expedited that year when I was asked to work with 17 first-grade classes in the Durham (North Carolina) City Schools. They had been notified *in October* that they had received a Right-to-Read grant from the Federal government.[5]

The reader should be aware that the program described in this book was not initiated under ideal conditions. It should have been difficult enough to ask teachers of 17 classes to stop doing what they had been doing and start a different program the next day. Most of the teachers, however, were willing to give it an honest try because they were neither satisfied with the way things had gone nor content with the reading/writing abilities of many of their students in the past. One teacher said she "boxed up things I'd been using for 20 years" and started this program the day after our first meeting. It took a few of the other teachers longer to break the traditional spells; however, as the program gradually unfolded, they, too, discarded some methods and materials in favor of this approach, and each added her own expertise to its dimensions.

Durham City Schools is an inner-city school district, supposedly populated with scores of youngsters destined for, if not already in, remedial classes. According to the proposal submitted by the Durham City Schools for the Right-to-Read grant, approximately 50 percent of all the students in grades 3 to 11 were below the 23rd percentile achievement level on the Science Research Associates reading test. Because such large numbers of black and white parents had put their children in private schools or had moved to other school districts, the Durham City Schools' 1969 enrollment of 14,101 had dropped to 9,389 in

[4]Paul Satz, "Reading Problems in Perspective." Also Wayne Otto, Nathaniel A. Peters, and Charles W. Peters, *Reading Problems: A Multidisciplinary Perspective* (Reading, Mass.: Addison-Wesley, 1977), pp. 43–44.

[5]This grant provided, among other items, the salaries for the additional first-grade teachers in the Durham City Schools classrooms. The opinions expressed in this book do not necessarily reflect the position or policy of the U.S. Office of Education, and no official endorsement by the U.S. Office of Education should be inferred.

1975. Of those who remained, approximately 80 percent were on government-subsidized lunches. Under these conditions, the program was begun in mid-October 1976, in approximately half of the first-grade classes. (Standardized test results achieved by these students after they were taught the *Success in Beginning Reading and Writing* program are found in Appendix Six.) At the end of the year, the teachers reported the total absence of nonreaders in their classes. No longer could the blame be placed completely on variables such as the students' homes, parents, vocabularies, and/or socioeconomic conditions.

The use of the program in the Wake County (North Carolina) class was the result of a conference in my office at Duke University with Mary S. Johnson, a doctoral student specializing in reading. Ms. Johnson had been an effective reading teacher in the Wake County Schools, but sudden withdrawal of salaries for reading teachers resulted in her becoming a first-grade teacher. She immediately grasped the concepts and program design and instituted the program. According to Ms. Johnson, all of the students in that class (half kindergarten and half first grade) were reading and writing by the end of the year.

All these teachers were aware of class performances in past years. Every year each teacher had in class a number of students who could not read or write with ease and enjoyment. Unfortunately, the same still holds true for most other first-grade teachers in this country. Blame should not be placed on these teachers. With the prevailing combinations of one teacher per classroom, materials, methods, and scheduling, it is simply an impossible task.

This book gives credit to the past efforts of educators and suggests an eclectic approach that synthesizes the strong points of many approaches. This book endorses the concept of professional teachers using a program that is open to the public, flexible in its internal components, yet structured in its design. In essence, it is a strong program for strong teachers.

The subtitle of this book is The Basal Concept of the Future. During the past five decades, basal readers used in the schools appeared as collections of short stories, poems, and so forth within attractive covers and were accompanied by a variety of supplementary materials, such as flash cards, workbooks, kits, and filmstrips. Accompanying these materials was a teacher's guide. Millions of dollars were spent on their production, and millions were spent on their purchase, as well as on other workbooks, kits, tapes, reading games, stencils, and the like.

The intent, apparently, was to package all the materials needed for beginning reading. The assumption was that by working through these materials the student would be able to tackle other reading materials. Those who would have learned to read anyway were confined by rigid compartmentalized "lessons." A great many more students failed to achieve any reading proficiency. Ultimately, it makes no difference whether a person can or cannot read the stories in a second- or fourth-grade basal reader. It does make a difference, however, if that person is able to read books, magazines, and newspapers, or anything else in print.

It is time to think of a basal concept in a much broader sense than simply sets of books and related materials. In *Success in Beginning Reading and Writing*, a basal program is viewed as any part of any material in print that appeals to youngsters—fiction, nonfiction, newspapers, magazines, textbooks, or even cereal boxes. The basal program of the future as described in this book expands rather than limits the reading lessons in the schools.

There is much talk of "humanizing" education. Perhaps one of the most humane things we can do for children is to give them an early confidence in reading and writing so they don't experience feelings of academic failure at age six or seven.

The program described in this book is a carefully designed combination of various educationally sound theories of reading instruction tied to realistic and practical ways to implement those theories so that each student can find success and motivation. The result is an exciting and challenging variety of learning experiences. The teacher and the program are teamed together to help the students. *What is taught, how it is taught, and what is learned in the early grades may be the most important part of the educational experience.*

We must continue to look to the schools for effective reading instruction. Those who have gained attention by criticizing the schools have not come up with workable alternatives. The basic premise of this book is that most first graders can learn to read and write and enjoy both by or before the end of the first grade. We must depend upon and support those administrators and teachers in this country who will accept this premise and work toward improving traditional approaches to the teaching of reading and writing. Educationally sound changes in attitude, program, scheduling, materials; and a renewed regard for the integrity of teachers and students will result.

Our generation can be the first to hear each first-grade child reading well and to see those students writing stories. Our generation can be the first to see to it that each first-grade child has taken several confident steps toward full reading and writing development. It will not, however, happen by accident.

Anne H. Adams
Duke University

Acknowledgments

I am grateful to the following people whose assistance and encouragement helped to make this book a reality:

To Dr. Benjamin T. Brooks, Superintendent of the Durham City Schools, who not only believes in logical and sound ideas for improving the instructional program but also implements such ideas in his schools;

To Dr. Frank Weaver, Associate Superintendent for Instruction of the Durham City Schools, who said he believed it could happen;

To Margaret Munford, Elementary Supervisor of the Durham City Schools, who worked so effectively in implementing the program;

To Joyce Wasdell, Assistant Superintendent for Instruction, and Elsa Woods, Coordinator of Reading, Durham County Schools, who provided administrative leadership;

To the principals of the schools in which the program was conducted, and especially to Bruce Benton, John Howard, William McCauley, Calvin Morgan, Dennis Nichols, Ruth Rogers, Janet Ruis, Patricia Sigler, Tommy Taylor, and William Woody;

To the teachers who were among the first to teach the program in 1976–1977 in the Durham City Schools: Hazel Bynum, Theresa Braswell, and Margaret Caple at Burton School; Roxie Stewart and Marcia Painter at East End School; Joyce Vestal, Nadine Hoover, and Angela Odom at R. N. Harris School; Madeline Malone, Lois Bryant, Glenda McMasters, Benita Buie, Margie Harrington, and Temple Jones at Lakewood School; Ruby McAllister, Mary Grant, and Carolyn Grant at Morehead School; Mary Childers, Laura Johnson, Linda Leonard, Delores Brown, Mamie Neal, and Brenda Bailey at W. G. Pearson School; and Edna Ellis, Annie Thompson, and Elizabeth Bowles at Watts Street School;

To the teachers, in addition to those named above, who taught the program in 1977–1978 in the Durham City Schools: Lynn Foushee, Betty Huffman, Emma King, and Brenda Skinner at R. N. Harris School; Betty Brunson, Louisa Douglass, Juanita Hedrick, and Minnie Packingham at Lakewood School; Mary Clayton and Nancy Stephens at Morehead School; Delois Brown, Paulette Bullock, Betty Cozart, Ann Davis, Ernestine Grady, Vanessa Gray, Patricia Hinnant, Janetta Holman, Frances Long, Marcia Riley, Rhonda Usner, and Josephine White at Pearson School; and Hilda Bell, Dora Green, Mary Harward, Selena Hunter, and Inez Rogers at Watts Street School;

To Mary Johnson who taught the program at Swift Creek School in Wake County;

To the teachers who taught the program in the Durham County Schools: Ann Dillon at Glenn School; Maxine Brown at Hillandale School; Susan Dobson, Carolyn Kirkland, Diane Liles, Becky Malone, and

Marcia Wender at Hope Valley School; Margaret Hayes at Little River School; and Pat Womack at Mangum School;

To members of the Durham City Schools Board of Education who visited the classes and endorsed the program: Josephine Clement, John Lennon, Harry Rodenhizer, and Dr. Theodore Speigner, Chairman;

To the following visitors who took the time to observe some of the classes and whose comments encouraged me to continue working on the program concept: The Honorable Terry Sanford, President of Duke University and former Governor of North Carolina; Dr. Anne Flowers, Chairperson of the Department of Education, and Dr. Robert Pittillo, Associate Professor in that department at Duke University; The Honorable James Green, Lieutenant Governor of North Carolina; Betty Owen, Special Advisor for Education Programs in the Office of the Governor of North Carolina, The Honorable James Hunt; Mary Purnell, Director of the Division of Reading, North Carolina State Department of Public Instruction, and Vickey Freitag, Consultant in that division; Anna Bass, Supervisor of Alamance County Schools; Dr. Judy Connors, Director of Reading, Greensboro Public Schools; Gladys Darensburg, Supervisor, Vance County Schools; Ken Yamomoto, Chief Planner for Reading for the State of Hawaii; The Honorable Charles Campbell, Educator and Representative, State of Hawaii;

To David Grady and Janice Gallagher, editors at Goodyear Publishing Company;

To the teachers, administrators, and parents who visited the classes;

To Dr. William Brown, Director, Division of Research, North Carolina Department of Public Instruction who provided assistance in the research design;

To Lou Bonds, Cornelia Olive, and Kathy McPherson of the Durham *Herald-Sun* newspaper who wrote perceptive features about the program;

To Elna Spaulding and William Bell, Durham County Commissioners who visited some of the classes;

To the following members of the North Carolina General Assembly who visited the classes: Representative J. P. Huskins, Senator Robert Jordan III, Senator Carolyn Mathis, Senator Ed Renfrow, Senator Kenneth Royall, Senator Willis Wichard, and Senator John Winters;

To Dr. James Sawyer, Director of Membership and Council Relations, International Reading Association, whose discussions with me during 1972–1976 helped shape some of the theories in this book;

To Alma Teeple, President of the North Carolina Association of Educators; and to Glenn Keever, Editor, *North Carolina Education,* who discussed with me the ideas underlying the concept of the professional teacher as presented in the book;

To the interns in the Duke University Reading Center who taught many of the lessons prior to their use in the schools;

To Marsha Bumphus, Donna Manji, and Jackie Ward who typed the manuscript;

To Dr. Michael Michlin, Dr. Sandra Robinson, Gordon Stanley, and Mary Frances Peete who read the manuscript; and especially to Helen Cappleman, who checked and double-checked to make sure the ideas were presented as accurately as possible.

chapter one
Objectives

THE BASIC ASSUMPTION

Success in Beginning Reading and Writing is based on the belief that people should be taught to read and to write about the kinds of materials that are and will be available to them in the future—fiction and nonfiction books, textbooks, newspapers, catalogues, maps, poems, magazines, telephone books, letters, brochures, and so on—in their natural form.

Once we recognize this assumption, we immediately reject the numerous so-called instructional materials that are counterproductive to success in learning to read and write and that also tend to retard rather than promote a child's comprehension of many different kinds of printed materials.

THE GENERAL OBJECTIVES

The three overall objectives in this program are:

1. *Reading* in the cognitive area
2. *Writing* in the cognitive area
3. *Positive self-concept* in the affective area

Some people equate reading ability with a standardized test score or with how well a student reads from a grade-level basal reader. In this program, the definition of *reading* is not limited to students' test scores or their reading from books on graded levels. Instead, reading is viewed as the process of an individual's progress in gaining information from a variety of printed sources in a purposeful and enjoyable manner. The process as developed in the program includes the transition from decoding sounds of alphabet symbols in words to expansion into a variety of styles of reading.

This program defines *writing* as both the mechanics of letter formation and the student creation of a variety of kinds of writing. A positive *self-concept* comes, in part, from successful academic endeavors in reading and writing.

SPECIFIC READING OBJECTIVES

An academic year consists of approximately 180 days, and the major assumption and each objective of this program should be realized each day. Each day's instructional program should include specific activities directed toward each child's meeting the goal;

however, direction is necessary in designing such lessons to produce successful results.

There are six specific objectives to be achieved individually and collectively based on the major assumption about reading.

Library Books

By the end of the year, every first grader will have read or tried to read at least 300 library books. This first objective alone marks this program as singularly different from all others. The number 300 is to provide a guide for teachers, students, and parents. Since some students will read more than 300 trade books and other students will read less than 300 books, we should not view the number as a limitation, nor should we use it as a pressure tool. All students in class, however, should have the opportunity to physically handle and try to read at least 300 library books.

It is extremely important to establish early in a person's life a pleasant attachment to printed stories and to seek the real source or book rather than an abbreviated version. This habit should be established in the first grade, and it is the school's responsibility to provide sufficient time, book resources, and instruction during the school year to enable every first grader to become addicted to library books.

The elementary students in a 1975 study indicated they watch television for approximately five hours per *school* day, eight hours on Saturday, and four hours on Sunday.[1] Because it is highly unlikely that the television habit will decrease, it is essential that blocks of time be scheduled in school to help develop a reading habit.

We cannot assume all of today's parents voluntarily can or will encourage their children to read. However, we can hope that if the school does this job well, today's children will take greater steps to make sure *their* children discover reading.

Textbooks

By the end of the year, every first grader will have read or tried to read many different kinds of primary-level textbooks. The second objective

[1]Anne H. Adams and Cathy B. Harrison, "Using Television to Teach Specific Reading Skills," *The Reading Teacher*, October 1975, p. 46.

strongly emphasizes first graders' reading in the content areas, such as mathematics, science, social studies, and health, as well as in music and art. One of the major concerns of upper-elementary-level teachers (as well as junior high and senior high school teachers) is the problems their students have in reading textbooks. Children should learn to read successfully subject-area textbooks—not just books and worksheets designed to teach them to read—without delay. Teachers should give specific reading and writing lessons using subject-area textbooks, beginning in the first grade.

Introduction to textbook reading is an integral and essential part of this program. In first-grade classrooms where mathematics, science, and social studies textbooks and workbooks are scarce, teachers should check the school's book room for any content-area books *for grades one to six* that are not being used and should requisition these books for use in the first-grade classes. They should not be intimidated by grade levels on the books.

By the end of the first grade, each child should have written both literal and interpretative answers after reading different kinds of subject-area(s) information. Literal answers will be written responses to such questions as who, what, when, and where—and the same answer can be found in print in the textbook. Interpretative answers to textbook information will concentrate on why and how, and students will apply their own analysis of information, interpret cause/effect relationships, make predictions, draw conclusions, and engage in other, higher-level reading, writing, and thinking skills.

Newspapers

By the end of the year, every first grader will be reading a daily newspaper. The third objective of this program recognizes the newspaper as a significant reading material, containing many of the words children hear on television and in their homes. The newspaper remains one of the few materials containing a large amount of printed matter relatively inexpensively. Unfortunately, there are adults, as well as children, who cannot, or do not, read the newspaper, thereby missing not only current and historical news reports but also economic information, such as sales. To augment televised news reports and simply to keep informed, people (even first graders) should be aware of the variety of information newspapers contain.

In addition to different types of printed information, newspapers present a variety of shapes and sizes of letters. In this program, reading skills ordinarily taught in conjunction with basal readers and supplementary readers are taught instead with newspapers, magazines, textbooks, library books, and other kinds of material in efforts to broaden the scope of reading instruction.

Catalogues

By the end of the year, every first grader will have read information in a variety of catalogues, printed forms, labels, boxes, and so on. The emphasis in this objective is, again, on relevancy and interest as well as on developing abilities to read materials that will be encountered during students' lifetimes. In this program there are specific lessons concerning a wide range of materials containing print—from cereal boxes to catalogue information.

Magazines

By the end of the year, every first grader will be reading different kinds of information in a variety of magazines. The magazine is a unique type of reading material, representing general information as well as specific emphases. Lessons are included in this program to introduce students to the variety of information in three types of magazines: children's magazines, such as *Sesame Street* and *Jack and Jill,* special-interest magazines, such as *Sports Illustrated* and *National Geographic,* and general-interest magazines, such as *Ebony* and *People.*

The students will write, cut, and paste on the magazine pages; therefore, magazines allocated for the school library cannot be used in this program as consumable items.

Comic Books

By the end of the year, every first grader will have read a variety of comic books. Comic books contain more reading aids than any other kind of printed matter. Such helps to reading include, but are not limited to:

1. Illustrations
2. "Balloons" indicating which conversations are made by which characters
3. Heavy shades of print indicating emphasized language
4. Fast-paced action
5. A variety of reading difficulty levels
6. Capsules of story plot placed in individual comic frames

Even with these advantages and the fact that most youngsters are interested in reading comics, the comics should be considered supplementary to the library books. There is no reason, however, to exclude them. In this program, the students can mark letters, words, and phrases in the comics as well as in the newspapers and magazines. Students apparently do not want the comics cut or torn.

SPECIFIC WRITING OBJECTIVES

There are two specific objectives to be achieved individually and collectively with the reading objectives based on the major assumption about writing.

Writing Stories

By the end of the year, every first grader will have written many different kinds of stories. Each of the stories, beginning with the very first "story" (which might be poorly formed alphabet letter symbols), should be kept in a manila folder containing the student-writer's name. Each story should be dated, at first by the teacher and as soon as possible by the student. The folders containing the stories *should not be sent home* until the end of the academic year. It is essential that students, teachers, administrators, supervisors, and parents have a complete record of each child's progress throughout the year. Students will detect many errors made earlier in the year as they review their stories filed from previous lessons. Other written work may be sent home, if so desired by the teacher; however, all of the stories from the language experience lessons should remain intact in each child's folder.

In a sense, one word can relay a story. Whether they consist of one word, several paragraphs, or several chapters, these stories should be viewed as the children's work. Although teachers should refer to positive ways to improve a part of a story, they should not write on children's story pages unless to make an encouraging comment. Teachers will have many other papers to mark while correcting. The stories from this segment of the program will give students a base from which to recognize errors or ways to improve story content. They also serve as a longitudinal record.

Other Writing Styles

In addition to stories, by the end of the year every first grader will have had the opportunity to write forms, memos, poems, letters, lists, and other forms of written communication. Teachers should also date these items when they are completed and file them in the students' language experience folders. Cardboard boxes can be used to hold folders that have been filed alphabetically according to the students' last names.

SPECIFIC AFFECTIVE OBJECTIVES

There are three specific objectives to be achieved individually and collectively with the reading and writing objectives based on the major assumption about the affective domain.

Achievement with Pride

By the end of the year, each first grader will have a sense of pride in his or her ability to read and write rather than the sense of frustration that occurs when poor achievers recognize other students can read and write with ease and enjoyment while they experience difficulty and failure.

Learning

By the end of the year, every first grader will be interested in learning and not afraid of it. All students should experience the desire to seek continued successful experiences while going through the learning process that are realized daily by students who do well in academics. All students should experience this sense of accomplishment.

Positive Self-Concept

By the end of the year, every first grader will have some sense of the power that comes with the ability to read and write successfully although many may not be able to express it verbally. This is an integral part of a positive self-concept, because students can discover things for themselves.

Overview of Program Components

The objectives set out in Chapter One will not happen in first grade classes by accident or with only incidental instruction. The importance of selection, implementation, and development of instructional components in this program cannot be underestimated. Both students who experience repeated successes in learning and teachers who observe growth in their students' abilities have strong positive feelings about their worth in the academic world.

A LESSON

In *Success in Beginning Reading and Writing*, each daily *lesson* is scheduled for $2\frac{1}{2}$ hours and consists of five different modules. Appendices One through Four contain the 174 lessons in the program.

There are usually 180 days in an academic year; however, the program details outlined below include 174 lessons, since standardized testing, field trips, and so on, may present a different kind of activity during the $2\frac{1}{2}$ hours.

Teachers have a variety of planning styles. The sequence of lessons is given on a daily basis, and teachers should compile the appropriate number of lessons in a manner they find meaningful.

THE MODULES WITHIN A LESSON[1]

Each of the five *modules* in a daily lesson represents a different, yet essential, aspect of teaching reading and writing. Although different in design, content, and focus, the modules reinforce each other to the extent that when taught together to form a lesson, they present a balanced reading/writing instruction program.

The five divisions or modules in the first lesson of Appendix One are: (1) Phonics/Spelling, (2) Language Experience, (3) Academic, Cultural Arts, and Current Events Reading, (4) Patterning, and (5) Recreational Reading. Each module should be scheduled for approximately 30 minutes (5 modules $\times$ 30 minutes = $2\frac{1}{2}$-hour lesson).

Appendices One through Four are intended both to aid teachers in planning instruction and to provide a tangible guide for parents, students, and other interested people in understanding what is going on in the classroom.

---

[1]Teachers who have students for less than $2\frac{1}{2}$ hours should divide the teaching period into five equal sections and teach each module daily.

LESSON 1

Introductory Phonics/Spelling—b

Write on chart paper words suggested by the students that contain b. Pronounce each word. Students write the letter b and words containing b. Discuss the meanings.

Examples: bat, job, banana, bumble bee, umbrella, box, basket, broom, boat.

Date and file each student's paper. Display the chart in the classroom.

FIRST 30 MINUTES IN LESSON

Language Experience—*Self: Things I Like*

Write on the chalkboard words suggested by students concerning things they like. Students begin writing sentences that begin "I like . . ."

Examples of vocabulary: *big birds, go-carts, bicycles, hamburger, puppies, my mama, spaghetti, friends.*

Date and file each student's paper.

SECOND 30 MINUTES IN LESSON

Academic, Cultural Arts, and Current Events Reading—Newspapers: b and c

Each student cuts or tears different shapes of the letters b and c from newspapers. They paste or tape the letters on their paper.

Check each student for b and c recognition.

Date and file the papers.

THIRD 30 MINUTES IN LESSON

Patterning—bă

Write on chart paper different endings for words beginning with bă.

Examples: bad, bat, bang, bathtub.

Stress Emphasis: Vocal stress on one word near beginning of sentences.

Display the chart in the classroom.

Student-Made Material: Each student draws a baseball bat and selects some of the words to write in the bat. Students use this material with other students.

FOURTH 30 MINUTES IN LESSON

Recreational Reading—Library Books

Help individual students find and pronounce words in library books that contain b.

FIFTH 30 MINUTES IN LESSON

6

Within each module there are reading skills, themes, and/or materials suggested as basic guides for inclusion in that module. The *teacher* decides how the guide should be developed in a particular classroom, and this decision is based on professional judgment. For example, in the Phonics/Spelling and Patterning Modules from Lessons 1–90, a daily suggestion of a way to change the presentation of each sound-symbol emphasis is made. These ideas should be considered only as suggestions and need not be followed exactly. If a teacher does not want to pop popcorn in Lesson 21, he or she should substitute some other attention-getting idea. A theme is suggested in each Language Experience Module, a reading skill emphasis in each Academic, Cultural Arts, and Current Events Reading Module, and a decoding emphasis in each Recreational Reading Module. Teachers may wish to substitute themes, word analyses, or comprehension skill emphases, depending on classroom situations. Although substitution and modification are encouraged, the modules should not be eliminated. The point is to teach the lesson component in a way that appeals to the students. In addition to inspiring interest, the idea or device serves as a cue to help students remember the module concept.

Although there are advantages in providing structure with some degree of flexibility in teaching this program, one caution is needed. *Skipping or reducing any module weakens the entire program* not only in the content that students should receive that day but also by giving some students the idea that greater importance is assigned to something other than their getting module instruction and doing a good job in completing it. All modules are important, and the absence of any segment not only weakens the entire program but also results in lower achievements, especially by those students who most need the lessons. For example, eliminating the Recreational Reading Module or including it only two or three days during the academic week instead of each day will not give students maximum time needed to finish large numbers of books. Eliminating or decreasing the Patterning Module lessons will not afford the back-up and the enrichment lessons necessary for success reinforcement in reading, writing, and spelling. Deleting or skipping Language Experience Modules will deprive students of opportunities to improve their creative writing abilities. If the Academic, Cultural Arts, and Current Events Reading

Modules are reduced in number, the students probably will not learn to read newspapers, magazines, and academic textbooks with comfort and enjoyment.

Many of the modules in the appendices contain guide examples. Most of these examples were volunteered by first-grade inner-city students who were taught this program. The examples should *not* become "core vocabulary" for this program just as Chart 7 in this chapter, which was developed in one first-grade class, should not be reproduced for other classes.

MAJOR PHASES IN THE PROGRAM

There are four phases of instruction in this program for the academic year. Each phase builds on the concepts and skills previously introduced, and no phase is ever completely eliminated. For example, when Phase 2 is introduced, Phase 1 emphasis continues, although its content and time decrease to provide time for Phase 2 components.

Phase 1

Phase 1 begins on the first day of school and receives total emphasis for the first ten lessons (days) of the academic year. The following components are essential in this phase of the program:

1. Establish a 2½-hour lesson and break it into five segments of approximately 30 minutes each.
2. Introduce a different letter and/or review a letter each day.
3. Introduce reading and writing teacher- and/or class-volunteered *words* containing the letters introduced or reviewed.
4. Make charts containing selected words studied and display the charts in the classroom. (These are not picture charts.) Use masking tape to put a sheet of chart paper on the chalkboard. Write the words on this paper. Hang the chart in the classroom, and display it for the remainder of the year.
5. Introduce a variety of materials containing print in conjunction with the teaching of those words.
6. Introduce knowledge-area themes. Establish class

conduct guidelines for each lesson, especially quiet time for reading during the Recreational Reading Modules.

Phase 1 lessons are found in Appendix One.

Phase 2

Phase 2 begins with the eleventh lesson (day of school) and continues along with Phase 1-type input through Lesson (day) 62. Phase 2 does not replace Phase 1. Introduction and review of alphabet letters and reading and writing of single words continue. The following components are essential in this phase of the program:

1. Introduce the concept of word *clusters*.
2. Instead of selecting single words only, teachers write two to five word clusters on the chart paper that are meaningful and that have been volunteered by students in the class. At least one word in each cluster must contain one of the letters being introduced or reviewed for that day's lesson.
3. Underline the letter emphasized in the lesson each time it appears in the cluster. Examples of word clusters from different lessons are: desk in the doorway, going home, red sunset, out of the house, incidentally speaking, play the game.
4. Have the students write some of the clusters and practice reading as many of them as possible.
5. Reinforce the concept of learning to read any cluster of words in each of the five modules in a lesson. For example, during the teacher–student conference in the Recreational Reading Modules, the student locates and reads not only some words that contain the element suggested for that day's lesson but also at least one of the words before and/or after this word.
6. Introduce knowledge-area themes.

Phase 2 lessons are found in Appendix Two.

Phase 3

Phase 3 begins with Lesson 63 and continues along with Phase 1 (single-word study) and Phase 2 (word clusters) through Lesson 90. In Phase 3 lessons, attention is still given to noting the specific letter(s) in single words and in word clusters. In addition, the instructional emphasis is directed toward reading *sentences* and *paragraphs*. Obviously, reading sentences and paragraphs will have been included earlier in the year; the difference now is in the lesson focus.

During Phase 3

1. Direct students' attention to detecting the power, purpose, and impact of various kinds of sentences.
2. Lead students to begin to understand purposes and development of paragraphs.
3. Introduce knowledge-area themes.
4. By the end of Phase 3, students should be able to cope with different kinds and lengths of sentences and paragraphs within stories, articles, and chapters.

Phase 3 lessons are found in Appendix Three.

Phase 4

Phase 4, the Expansion Phase, includes Lessons 91–174. This phase is explained in Chapter Eight and contains certain modifications of the earlier parts of the program. Although the $2\frac{1}{2}$-hour instructional block is maintained, the Patterning Module is deleted. The Recreational Reading Module is lengthened to one hour.

1. Emphasize reading and writing complete stories and chapters.
2. Stress various interpretations of items read.
3. Emphasize syllabication and other forms of structural analysis in the Phonics/Spelling Modules.
4. Introduce knowledge-area themes.
5. Expand the Language Experience Module to include writing letters, poems, and factual information. Encourage students to select their *own* topics for story writing.

6. Stress reading other kinds of material, such as catalogues, telephone books, maps, and forms, as well as reading to locate specific information and interpretative reading.

Phase 4 lessons are found in Appendix Four. Table 1 shows the development of the five modules within the four phases.

MINIMUM TIME ALLOCATIONS

This daily 2½ hours of the reading/writing program should begin on the first day of school; however, if that day is filled with record-keeping and other non-instructional matters, begin the program on the second school day.

Since each module represents at least 30 teaching minutes, it is necessary for each teacher to move instruction from one module to the next module with facility and ease as one 30-minute period elapses and another begins. The time suggestions for each module may lead some people to believe this program rushes, pushes, or pressures students. This is not the program's intent. Instead, within each 30-minute module, each student should experience success with some or all aspects of that lesson. Students are never expected to experience success with everything in the lesson within the 30-minute span. Students should not be expected or persuaded to complete a story in one Language Experience Module. Instead, each student should experience some success within the story-writing lesson. This does not necessarily mean the story should be finished. It can be finished later, if the student so desires.

Under no circumstances should one 30-minute module consume an hour at the expense of another

TABLE 1   Modules in the Four Phases

	PHASE 1	PHASE 2	PHASE 3	PHASE 4
Phonics/ Spelling	Single letters are studied in any position in a word. Students give *one word* examples.	Single letters are studied in any position in a word. Student examples are *clusters* of words containing the letter studied.	Single letters and groups of letters are studied in words. Student examples are *sentences* with words containing the letter(s) studied.	Letters and groups of letters are studied with emphasis on multisyllabic words. Student examples are *paragraphs* containing these.
Language Experience	Stories with assigned themes			Stories about subject of student's choice, memos, poems, letters, factual information, etc.
Academic, Cultural Arts, and Current Events Reading	Magazines, newspapers, and content-area textbooks			Additional reading of maps, telephone books, forms, and catalogues
Patterning	Groups of words containing letter or letter clusters in the same position			Module deleted
Recreational Reading	Independent reading of library books, with assigned letter or topic. Individual conferences with teacher.			Module increased to one hour, conferences continue.

9

module. Among the benefits of providing a minimum of 30 minutes for each module are that:

1. Students begin to learn how to budget their time to complete work within a given slot—an extremely important study skill.
2. Thirty minutes affords enough time in each module for both reading and writing instruction and for application of lesson ingredients for every student in the class.
3. Each student has enough time to experience closure and success in completing some work in each of five instruction sessions. Students also realize that they can do more. These two items—closure and future implications—are keystones in good learning situations.

A fire drill or some other emergency is the only thing that should interrupt any module's instruction for the entire class.

Teachers have expressed two major concerns about the five 30-minute modules: (1) 30 minutes is too long at the beginning of the year, and (2) 30 minutes is not long enough for some of the modules (especially the Language Experience Module and cutting/pasting activities in the Academic, Cultural Arts, and Current Events Module toward the end of the year). Some teachers allocated portions of the day other than 2½ hours for individuals to complete the work. Since there is more time to teach than the 2½ hours during the school day, only the teacher should decide to devote some of that time to the extension of this program or to other matters.

Each module should be taught in sequence—Phonics/Spelling; Language Experience; Academic, Cultural Arts, and Current Events Reading; Patterning; and Recreational Reading—at a prearranged time during the school day, so that administrators, parents, other visitors, and, especially, teachers and students will expect such instruction to be taking place. For example, if parents want to observe how their child is being taught phonics, they are advised that phonics instruction takes place during the first 30 minutes of the 2½-hour program. The teacher should post on the wall outside the classroom door the 2½-hour teaching schedule for each teacher using this program.

The following is an example of a class schedule to post outside the classroom door:

Phonics/Spelling	9:00–9:30
Language Experience	9:30–10:00
Academic, Cultural Arts, and Current Events Reading	10:00–10:30
Patterning	10:30–11:00
Recreational Reading	11:00–11:30

At a time of concern and questions about how and when reading is taught, this plan, followed honestly, is effective not only in assuring people that the schools can do the job effectively but also in opening the doors for intelligent observation of what is being done to teach reading and writing in a sensible and creative manner. There is no reason to fear scheduling times for certain components within an educational program. The 30 minutes for each module offer the flexibility of the "open-class" concept because teachers develop the content according to their expertise. On the other hand, the time-and-module focus affords a basic structure and direction that promotes assurance that a planned and educationally sound program is being taught each day to each child in the class.

MATERIALS DISTRIBUTION

There are several techniques for distributing materials that teachers should use to minimize lost time within the 30-minute modules. A large amount of time is wasted over an academic year if the scissors, paper, magazines, library books, newspapers, and so on are kept in one place in the classroom. Instead, there should be at least four stations for storing materials and at least four people to distribute the materials simultaneously. The materials in the stations can be kept in cardboard boxes. Although it seems a minor point, even the speed at which items are distributed for students to work with can become a critical element.

SKILLS

There is no predetermined sequence of reading skills even though specific reading skills are emphasized in the Academic, Cultural Arts, and Current Events Reading Modules, Patterning Modules, and Phonics/Spelling Modules. These skill topics are identified to aid teachers in focusing emphasis on reading skills while using different kinds of printed materials.

The skills needed to read and write whatever the lesson is about should be given priority in instruction. For example, if a newspaper article calls for a prediction, that skill should be emphasized. If a student does not capitalize the first word in a sentence written during the Language Experience Module, the teacher should call the student's attention to that skill, referring to that particular sentence. This method is the antithesis of the concept of identifying a skill and introducing it in an artificial manner.

Basic sight words are not taught from isolated lists or as "new" words. Sight words, such as *is, when, before,* and so on, should be taught as encountered in a sentence or paragraph in an individualized rather than collective approach.

READING COMPREHENSION

Unless they understand to some degree, students do not read as they move their eyes across printed lines. This program does not treat reading comprehension skills or activities as separate or artificial entities. There is a major difference in the approach to teaching reading comprehension in this program and in some other programs. In this program there are no predetermined meanings given to words that students must memorize to arrive at the "correct answer." Instead, the *Success in Beginning Reading and Writing* program fosters the concept of accepting that part of meanings expressed by students on that day and at that time of their education. Teachers then have the opportunity to help students gain additional information about the meanings.

For example, the following meanings were volunteered by first graders when asked by the teacher to define *tap:*

water faucet
things on shoes
touch somebody
put something in a tree
a dance
something on a telephone

Verbal communication is the keystone to gaining the students' voluntary answers. Teachers then direct students' attention to an understanding of the meaning of a word as it is found within a specific context. In the example, the sentence containing *tap* was: *Water was dripping because the tap was loose.*

During Lessons 1–90, teachers should make comprehension checks as frequently and as informally as possible as the students learn to decode words. For example, the question, What does this mean to you? is a good check for comprehension, since the same word is frequently interpreted differently (yet correctly) by different students. Under no circumstances should this kind of comprehension check be omitted or used infrequently.

Beginning with Lesson 91, teachers should use a more formalized approach to internal comprehension checks, referring to any kind of printed material used in any module (see Chapter Ten).

CHARTS[2]

The charts are very important and they represent one of the key elements in this program—student vocabulary. In fact, the charts are one of the obvious features to visitors to this program's classrooms.

The first chart is hung as soon as possible after the first lesson, and it contains words that (1) contain the letter b and (2) were suggested by the students. For the remainder of the academic year, charts should be displayed everywhere space is available—walls, bulletin boards, and doors, as well as strung on lines across the classroom. By the end of the year, over 200 charts should be displayed.

[2]The suggested size for the Phonics/Spelling charts is 24-inch-by-32-inch paper. The suggested size for the Patterning charts is 8-inch-by-11-inch paper.

11

Although the charts are written by the teacher, the contents of the chart come from the students' vocabularies. These are not picture charts, and they should not be made in advance of the module's instruction.

There are two major purposes in displaying many charts in the classroom:

1. They serve as a readily available reference with hundreds of words for students to use *at all times* when writing, but especially during the Language Experience Modules. Without the charts, students have very little to aid them in spelling.
2. They are always available for instant review purposes. Their content contains words familiar to students (since the students volunteered the words), and the teacher does not have to mimeograph words for review material.

Students should not be required to memorize each word on each chart. In all probability, no two classrooms will be displaying identical charts. These charts should not be confused with "basic sight word" lists. Sight words should be included where appropriate in the word clusters or sentences on the charts, not in isolated settings.

The charts are outgrowths of *each* Phonics/ Spelling Module and *each* Patterning Module. At the top of the chart, write the alphabet letter(s) emphasized in that lesson. Underline these *letters* wherever they appear in the words written on the charts from the Phonics/Spelling Modules. Underline the letters representing the same pattern taught in the Patterning Modules. Depending on which phase is underway, the charts contain words, word clusters, or sentences. Later in the year, the charts contain paragraphs developed in the lessons. The number or length of items written on a chart is left to the discretion of the teacher.

One of the interesting situations that develops during the chart development concerns the teachers' learning from their students. For example, since most of the students watch Saturday morning television cartoons (and most of the teachers do not), the teachers often find themselves writing on the charts the names of current cartoon characters and some of their antics. Another interesting factor is the growth of teachers' awareness of the ingenuity of their students in their abilities to associate word selections and meaning interpretations. For example, teachers report such unusual (for first grade) sentences as

I have dandru<u>ff</u> in my hair.

or

I like <u>H</u>ardee's <u>H</u>uskies.

Teachers usually look forward to hearing what their students volunteer in the next Phonics/Spelling and Patterning Modules. However, handling profanity or other "objectionable" words proposed by a student can be a problem. Teachers should use common sense if a student volunteers a word that is considered offensive or profane. It is best not to write those words on the board or charts, and teachers may have to explain that although these words are spoken by a great many people, they are usually not put in school textbooks for young children. This can be a sensitive matter, and teachers should consider how they will handle it in the event the occasion arises.

The following are examples of *phonics* charts that show how the chart content changes as the year progresses:

Lessons 1–10: Single words on charts, each word containing the letter emphasized in the Phonics/ Spelling Modules in any position (see Chart 1).

Lessons 11–62: Clusters of words; the letters emphasized in the Phonics/Spelling Modules are found in some, but not necessarily each word in each cluster (see Chart 2).

Lessons 63–90: Sentences incorporating some words that contain letters emphasized in the Phonics/Spelling Modules (see Chart 3).

Lessons 91–121: Sentences containing some two-syllable words that also contain letter clusters emphasized in the Phonics/Spelling Modules (see Chart 4).

Lessons 122–152: Sentences containing some three-syllable words that also contain letters emphasized in the Phonics/Spelling Modules (see Chart 5).

Lessons 153–168: Sentences containing some four-syllable words that also contain letter clusters emphasized in the Phonics/Spelling Modules (see Chart 6).

Lessons 169–end of academic year: Sentences containing some five-syllable words that also contain letter clusters emphasized in the Phonics/Spelling Modules (see Chart 7).

CHART 1 **Example of Phonics Chart from Lesson 1–10**

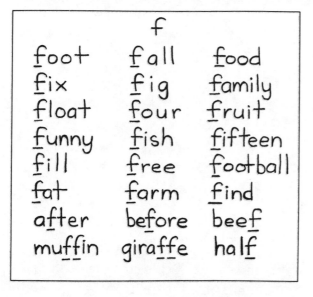

f

foot	fall	food
fix	fig	family
float	four	fruit
funny	fish	fifteen
fill	free	football
fat	farm	find
after	before	beef
muffin	giraffe	half

CHART 2 **Example of Phonics Chart from Lessons 11–62**

F

Fred Flintstone
Frosty the Snowman
Hawaii Five-O
Friday morning
Fat Albert
the month of February
my brother Freddie
the Fonz
Father's Day
Frankenstein monster
the state of Florida

13

CHART 3   Example of Phonics Chart from Lessons 63–90

br

I have a <u>br</u>other.
My mom sweeps with a <u>br</u>oom.
Do you have a <u>br</u>uise?
The magician said "A<u>br</u>acada<u>br</u>a!"
I eat <u>br</u>eakfast every morning.
He lives in a <u>br</u>ick house.
The soldier is <u>br</u>ave.
I read about Charlie <u>Br</u>own.
He <u>br</u>oke my toy.
I think with my <u>br</u>ain.
We visited the li<u>br</u>ary.

CHART 4   Example of Phonics Chart from Lessons 91–121

th

He has a <u>th</u>ousand dollars.
<u>Th</u>under frightens me.
My bro<u>th</u>er has a bir<u>th</u>day.
I have milk in my <u>th</u>ermos.
We are hot and <u>th</u>irsty.
She is <u>th</u>irteen years old.
Today is <u>Th</u>ursday.
I love my mo<u>th</u>er.
Birds have fea<u>th</u>ers.
Are you <u>th</u>inking?
The wea<u>th</u>er is cold
Sunday is the Sab<u>ba</u>th.

CHART 5   Example of Phonics Chart from Lessons 122-152

h

I eat Hardee's <u>h</u>am<u>b</u>urgers.
Bears <u>hibernate</u> in the winter.
What is <u>happening</u>?
I never <u>misbehave</u>.
They went on a <u>honeymoon</u>.
Do not <u>hesitate</u> to go.
I have a white <u>handkerchief</u>.
The sun comes over the <u>horizon</u>.
That liver tastes <u>horrible</u>.
We had a <u>Halloween</u> party.

CHART 6   Example of Phonics Chart from Lessons 153-168

s

I buy groceries at the <u>supermarket</u>.
A <u>security</u> guard protects us.
We watch "Spook <u>Spectacular</u>" on TV.
My mom bought a <u>Simplicity</u> pattern.
A <u>salamander</u> is like a lizard.
That <u>speedometer</u> goes up to 120.
The movie was <u>sensational</u>.
A <u>stenographer</u> works in an office.
Are you <u>sleepyheaded</u>?

CHART 7   Example of Phonics Chart from Lessons 169—end of year

t

He is sick with <u>tuberculosis</u>.
My dad belongs to an <u>organization</u>.
I know the <u>multiplication</u> tables.
That boy is <u>temperamental</u>.
She is our <u>representative</u>.
The doctor did a <u>tonsillectomy</u>.
It is <u>temporarily</u> out of order.
We are <u>redecorating</u> our house.

CHART 8   Example of Patterning Chart

−ick

pick
sick
tick
Rick
lick
quick
click
brick
thick
trick
stick

CHART 9   Example of Patterning Chart

oo

too	book
room	look
moon	foot
food	took
groovy	shook
racoon	stood
shampoo	crooked
kangaroo	brook
igloo	woodpecker

There is a basic difference in the items underlined on the patterning charts and those items highlighted on the phonics charts. Charts 8 and 9 are examples from Patterning Modules. Compare Chart 1 from a Phonics/Spelling Module with Chart 8 from a Patterning Module. In the Phonics/Spelling Modules, the position of the letter(s) does not matter; in the Patterning Modules, the position is extremely important.

VOCABULARY

In this program, students begin with words they have in their speaking vocabulary and proceed to learn new words volunteered by others in the class or found in print. The freedom to learn to read and write unlimited and uncontrolled vocabulary is an essential component in this program.

ACCOUNTABILITY

There is a difference between standardized testing and accountability. Although it is popular today to spend taxpayers' money and educational time on administering, scoring, recording, and filing test scores, this program requires a more realistic approach to assessment.

Teaching—Learning Accountability

In this program, accountability is based on observing what each student can and cannot read and write rather than on test scores or reading from a preassigned basal "level" book. Some of the accountability measures considered should be:

1. Records of student reading and writing activities kept in a separate manila folder *for each student each day*.
2. Class visitation opportunity every *day* during the 2½ hours for parents and other interested persons.

3. Teacher estimation of the
   a. number of nonreaders in the class (nonreader defined as a student not able to read *any* words).
   b. number of students reading at the beginning or first-grade stage.
   c. number of students reading above first-grade stage.
   d. number of students who cannot write even alphabet letters.
   e. number of students who can write.
4. Teacher indication of the number of library books (not textbooks) recorded in the classroom as read or examined by students.
5. Story written by *each student in the class* on blank stencils. The stencils should be reproduced and copies given to the parents and to each student in the class.

The Fallacy of "Reading Levels"

In this program, the professional teacher's opinion is important for determining the number of students who can't read at all, can read a little, and can read a lot. The value judgments of *at all, a little,* and *a lot* may be more meaningful than reading levels 1.3, 6.2, 5.7, etc.

For years, educators have been encouraged to pay attention to students' "reading level" even though the concept is confusing. For example, some people are concerned about the inconsistency of reading level or difficulty in the fifth grade basal readers and the fifth grade social studies textbooks. The importance given to "levels" should be reexamined, and improved ways should be found to assess what children can and cannot read in a myriad of printed materials.

TEACHERS

Finding ways to get students off to a successful start in reading and writing is more important than concentrating resources on later remediation. The traditional pattern has been to charge one teacher with the responsibility of initiating twenty-five to thirty-five six-year-olds to the world of academics. When some of these students did not achieve a certain level, remedial reading teachers were employed to help them in the upper grades. One result was the development of a kind of educational welfare system.

We should change our direction and employ a second professional teacher to help first graders for half of each school day while this program is taught. The class ratio is reduced by half, and each student's chances of achieving success are enhanced. Today's remedial reading teachers at the upper levels could be tomorrow's reading enrichment teachers.

Whether the state and/or school district will provide the resources to hire two certified elementary or reading teachers for at least part of each day in a first grade class depends on allocation of funds and whether the decision makers recognize the need for two certified teachers to reduce class pupil–teacher ratio. *A single first-grade teacher can teach all the lesson topics in this program.* The major difference is that one teacher will not have the time to work with as many students individually as can two teachers. One teacher cannot explain the lessons in detail as can two teachers.

Placing two certified teachers at least half of each day in the first-grade classrooms is economically feasible. It is not economically feasible to have two second-grade teachers in each second-grade class. However, students who move from this first-grade program into the traditional second grade may, as one principal said, find the second grade program "rather flat." School systems will have to concentrate on improving the second grades to accommodate students who like to read and are accustomed to reading a variety of materials. This is the dream of parents and dedicated educators—changing education because of success.

REVIEW

Success in Beginning Reading and Writing affords a series of built-in reviews, especially for phonics and reading/writing skills development. With the exception of the first few lessons in which the same letter(s) are included, the reviews take place not only on different days but also when students use a different kind of reading material on the same day.

This concept of review (1) avoids a sameness of instruction and alleviates student boredom and (2) presents the review material as an integral part of introduction to reading new materials.

Here is an example of the predominate review pattern in this program:

Learning to Read and Write Words Containing G

g	Lesson 7	Phonics/Spelling Module
g	Lesson 10	Phonics/Spelling Module
G, g	Lesson 13	Academic, Cultural Arts, and Current Events Reading Module
g	Lesson 16–18	Recreational Reading Module
gă	Lesson 19	Patterning Module
gŏ	Lesson 20	Patterning Module
gŭ	Lesson 21	Patterning Module
G	Lesson 55	Phonics/Spelling Module
gr	Lesson 71	Phonics/Spelling Module
ing	Lesson 77	Recreational Reading Module
dge	Lesson 86	Phonics/Spelling Module
gn	Lesson 86	Patterning Module
gh	Lesson 87	Phonics/Spelling Module
ng, ing	Lesson 88	Phonics/Spelling Module

In addition to these lessons in which g is specifically emphasized in a variety of ways, students will encounter g in words volunteered or found in print in all modules.

Under no circumstances is a letter introduced once and then ignored. Some students will grasp the concept early in the year and will feel comfortable as they decode with comprehension words containing that symbol. For other students, sufficient reviews of the symbol are built into the program to afford them at least ten opportunities to learn to decode that symbol. These ten lessons do not include the incidental appearance of the symbol in other lessons.

GROUPING

This program does not recommend the formation of small groups for reading instruction. Traditionally, classes are broken into three to five groups, and the teacher works with one group (usually in a circle) at a time. Such grouping practice is generally ineffective in reaching all students, places an undue physical drain on the teacher, and encourages the concept of "seat work" or "busy work."

The teacher actually has less time to help each child in a small group than when the students are at their desks and the teacher moves from individual to individual. In addition, in the small-group situation, the teacher is doing most of the work, while some of the students wait for "their turn" in the group.

The most disturbing aspect of the traditional program is that some students, identified early in the year, are placed in the "slow" group, from which many of them are never removed. The stigma attached to this is devastating and totally unnecessary.

The formation of small groups does not assure more individualized or improved teaching or learning. In this program, there are two major kinds of grouping: whole class and spontaneous peer-selected groups.

Whole-Class Grouping

Introductory remarks and module directions are presented at one time to the entire class. This is a part of the development of the listening-skills aspects in this program.

Peer-Selected Grouping

Development of the lesson is the responsibility of each individual student, who may seek assistance from the teacher or from other students in the class. When two or more students work together, they should form the group. Teachers decide on group members only when students abuse their privilege of selecting their workmates.

Advanced and Remedial Students

One of the most difficult, yet pleasant, aspects in this program is providing for those students who enter first grade with highly developed reading and writing skills and, at the same time, providing for students who cannot read and write at all, as well as for others whose abilities are between the two extremes. As in all other aspects, teachers armed with flexible and strong programs are the key to success.

Teachers do not have enough time or energy to teach two markedly different programs at the same time. Nor is it sound, or even practical, to put one group of students into a program that is unrelated to what the rest of the class is doing. This division of content is time consuming and, in general, frustrating to teachers and students.

The challenge is to develop a program that does not dwell on compartmentalization of students. The ability grouping concept does not work. For example, some "good" readers are "poor" spellers.

The first prerequisite to providing for all students in this program is to realize that two extremes of content can be included within the same lesson framework. Some specific examples are:

1. During the Phonics/Spelling Modules, "easy" as well as "difficult" words can be introduced, so there is an opportunity for *every* student to learn new words.

2. During the Language Experience Modules, advanced vocabulary and topics or concepts to write about can be included in the introductory portions amid easier content and vocabulary.

3. Students who can write should be encouraged to begin writing a story on the first day of school at the same time some of their less-able peers may just be learning how to hold a pencil.

4. The Phonics/Spelling and Patterning Modules provide a strong spelling base, and for this reason alone, advanced first graders should not be deprived of these lessons. Students just beginning to grasp the concept of selecting one letter to follow another in forming words obviously need both the Phonics/Spelling and Patterning Modules.

5. During the Academic, Cultural Arts, and Current Events Reading Modules, students can receive specific questions, such as "Can you underline one

problem mentioned in an editorial?" while some of their friends are still pasting letters on paper. Since almost all first graders enjoy the pasting lessons, advanced students should not be deprived of this kind of activity.

6. One of the greatest differences in program provisions for advanced first graders is in the reading of fiction and nonfiction. All students, but especially the advanced, should be encouraged to read or examine large numbers of books *of their choice* for enjoyment as well as for information. No matter what a student's ability, each book read or examined gives that student insights into new areas of learning. Students tend to select the kinds of books they feel comfortable with, if that freedom is granted them. In this program, *all* students are encouraged to become addicted to books.

The Severely Disabled Student

This program will not automatically equalize all students in academic abilities. If the program is followed, however, its components are designed to move the completely illiterate student into the beginnings of literacy. These students will not accomplish either the quantity or quality of work achieved by more advanced students within any given module. However, teachers should help these students accomplish *something* within each lesson.

Provision can be made for any student in the class, simply by adjusting the level of the vocabulary and the assignment. This can be done only by the teacher in collaboration with the students. It is best to make different provisions for all students within the framework of one overall program design. Each module can be directed to reach students in need of remedial instruction or directed to interest advanced students. This is one essence of flexibility in selecting instruction content. Grouping, therefore, is accomplished without an overt showing of its presence.

chapter three
The Phonics/Spelling Module

PURPOSE

The Phonics/Spelling Modules are intended to teach students strategies necessary to decode with comprehension any word in the language that they wish to read. By beginning with words students bring to school in their speaking vocabularies, the elements of guessing or fear of trying to read certain words are reduced. Writing activities are coupled with reading as reinforcements in learning so the students learn to read and write simultaneously.

SCHEDULING

This program contains 174 Phonics/Spelling Modules. Suggestions for teaching each of these modules are found in Appendices One through Four. The first 30 minutes of the 2½-hour block is devoted to phonics instruction, and each Phonics/Spelling Module emphasizes a letter or cluster of letters within words. The first module should begin as soon as possible after the beginning of school.

In each of the first three phonics modules, a new letter is introduced. After Lesson 3, Introductory Modules and Review Modules are alternated each day. This continues until Lesson 51. In Lessons 52–90, an Introductory Module and a Review Module are included in each Phonics/Spelling Module. Lessons 91–174 review letters or letter clusters previously introduced; however, multisyllabic words are stressed. Table 2 shows the alphabet sequence in the Phonics/Spelling Modules.

GUIDELINES FOR CONTENT SELECTION

In the Phonics/Spelling Modules, the procedure includes selecting words that contain the preidentified letter(s) somewhere within the words, drawing the students' attention to that part of the word, noting its relationship to the rest of the word, and discussing in recitation or in writing some possible meanings of the words.

TABLE 2 Suggested Phonics Plan*

LESSON	INTRODUCTORY PHONICS	REVIEW PHONICS	LESSON	INTRODUCTORY PHONICS	REVIEW PHONICS
1	b	—	46	—	e, y
2	c	—	47	o	—
3	d	—	48	—	i, z
4	—	b, c	49	u	—
5	f	—	50	—	o, a
6	—	d	51	A, B	—
7	g	—	52	C	e, i
8	—	f, b	53	D, E	—
9	h	—	54	F	u, A
10	—	g, c	55	G, H	B
11	j	—	56	I	C, D
12	—	h, d	57	J, K	E
13	k	—	58	L	F, G
14	—	j, f	59	M, N	H
15	l	—	60	O	I, J
16	—	k, g	61	P, Qu	K
17	m	—	62	R	L, M
18	—	l, h	63	S, T	N
19	n	—	64	U	O, P
20	—	m, j	65	V, W	Qu
21	p	—	66	X, Y, Z	R
22	—	n, k	67	br	S, T
23	q	—	68	bl	U
24	—	p, l	69	cr, dr	V
25	r	—	70	fl	W, br
26	—	q, m	71	fr, gr	X, Y
27	s	—	72	gl, pl	Z
28	—	r, n	73	pr, sm	bl
29	t	—	74	sl, tr	cr
30	—	s, p	75	sc, scr	dr
31	v	—	76	sp, spl	fl
32	—	t, q	77	st, str	fr
33	w	—	78	sk, sn	gr
34	—	v, r	79	sh, shr	gl
35	x	—	80	ch	pl
36	—	s, w	81	th, thr	pr
37	y	—	82	qu, squ	sm
38	—	x, t	83	sw, wh	sl
39	z	—	84	ph	tr
40	—	y, v	85	wr	scr
41	a	—	86	dge, tch	sc
42	—	z, w	87	nd, gh	spl
43	e	—	88	ng, ing	sp
44	—	a, x	89	ck	str
45	i	—	90	cl	st

*Lessons 91–121 emphasize two-syllable words containing previously introduced letters. Lessons 122–152 emphasize three-syllable words containing previously introduced letters. Lessons 153–168 emphasize four-syllable words containing previously introduced letters. Lessons 169–174 emphasize five-syllable words containing previously introduced letters.

22

The Alphabet as a Management System

In *Success in Beginning Reading and Writing*, there are no separate lessons emphasizing learning the *names* of the alphabet letters (A, B, C, D, etc.), and there are no lessons in which students draw or match geometric shapes. The alphabet (names of letters) is used only as a convenient organizational tool from which module topics are developed. In fact, from the very beginning of this program and throughout its entirety, an alphabet letter or letter cluster is selected to provide students with the *opportunity* to see all letters in *all* kinds of combinations, restricted only by the words students select. The object is to learn letters in conjunction with their function in the structure of words, not just to memorize the alphabet.

Using b as the first alphabet stimulus in the Phonics/Spelling Module and following it with the alphabet consonant sequence before introducing the vowels is arbitrary. Although program users have found no problems with this sequence, there are other kinds of sequences teachers might wish to use: (1) begin with a (Lesson 41) and follow the alphabet sequence, (2) introduce the alphabet according to sequence based on the difficulty of the sound formations (the sounds of b and m, for example, are usually easier to pronounce than the sounds of w and r), (3) introduce alphabet letters according to those that have similar writing strokes (g and p would be taught at a different time in the sequence from t and f), or (4) any other logical sequence. The ideas in the appendices are applicable, no matter which day a letter is introduced. Regardless of the sequence, teachers should not skip any of the letters children have to deal with in both reading and in writing.

Student-Centered Vocabulary Selections

One of the unique and best aspects of this program is the unlimited freedom provided to each class in the selection of vocabulary studied. There is no controlled vocabulary, no predetermined selection of words to be learned. All of the words used in the Phonics/Spelling Modules come from students, supplemented by words in print. Some reading programs have been criticized severely because some of the vocabulary used was not meaningful to the students. This criticism does not apply to this program.

Whether the students are in inner-city, educationally disadvantaged classrooms, in affluent classrooms, or in remote rural areas, the vocabulary for most of their reading/writing lessons in this module is selected from their word knowledge or from an ever-changing student selection of printed materials, with assistance from the teacher.

There are, however, basic guidelines to use in selecting vocabulary for study. The words used in the Phonics/Spelling Modules should

1. Contain the alphabet symbol(s) identified for emphasis in the module.
2. Be selected by the *students* from their speaking vocabulary.

Only in instances in which the students cannot volunteer examples should teachers pronounce and write examples on the chalkboard from their own personal vocabulary or from the examples provided in each Phonics/Spelling Module. The first option to identify words should be given to the students.

During Lessons 1–10 the teacher writes one-word examples containing the letter(s) studied and suggested by the students. Beginning with Lesson 11, clusters of words are given and recorded on the charts. At least one word in the cluster should contain the letter(s) studied. This continues until Lesson 63. At that time all student examples should be complete sentences containing words with the letter(s) studied.

If teachers are not completely certain of the spelling of some words volunteered orally by students, they should consult a dictionary rather than exclude the word from the chalkboard. Teachers using a dictionary remind the students that everyone cannot spell every word and must check it in a dictionary. In fact, students need to observe their teachers using a dictionary. This model may encourage the students to use a dictionary when they need to be assured of a spelling.

The letter(s) to be emphasized is identified at the beginning of each Phonics/Spelling Module, along with a few words or word clusters containing the letter(s). *Students should not memorize these word examples.* Instead, they are models, and *students should watch as the teacher writes the words.* These examples should be used only as backup examples in the event students cannot verbally identify a sufficient number of examples of words or word clusters containing the symbols. If students identify enough words, it will not be necessary to use the words listed in each Phonics/Spelling Module in the appendices.

Teachers should not judge the word selection. When children are offered an unlimited variety of words and are not restricted by their teachers to the words found in "easy" reading selections, many students prefer "long words" to a steady diet of pap words. *As long as adults decide something is too hard for a first grader, that student is deprived of the opportunity to learn it.* The only stipulations should be that the example must contain the letter(s) emphasized in the module, and under no circumstances should words that are totally unfamiliar to every student in the class be placed on the chalkboard or charts. Especially after Lesson 91, the students look forward to decoding longer and longer words. This is one reason for the emphasis on two-to-five-syllable words in the Expansion Phase (see Chapter Eight).

Sound–Symbol Association

Do not assign any predetermined sound to a given letter(s). *When we read, we never know which words are ahead and what pronunciation will be necessary to decode those words.* For example, note the different placement and sounds given the letters a, s, and t in this sentence and the next sentence. For this reason, it is imperative that students associate the decoding process within words encountered in the module rather than in an artificially structured situation. The object is to teach them to cope successfully with *any* letter combinations within *any* words at *any* given time, because the final objective is to enable them to read real materials in the real world.

Phonics rules should not be taught. Instead, students should be helped to work with sounds or notice the absence of sounds in words presented in each phonics module. Another unique aspect of this program is the teaching of phonic sounds according to their presence in words rather than according to the letter(s). The emphasis is always on immediate application of phonics.

Spelling–Writing Emphasis

Students writing during the Phonics/Spelling Module should be encouraged to select from the examples given by the class those words, clusters, or sentences they want to write in addition to words not on the charts.

Students should not be expected to spell large numbers of words. However, teachers should introduce them to the concept that certain letters follow other letters to create words.

Introduction to spelling is built into this program because the students watch the teacher write words on the chart paper. Any additional emphasis given to spelling is left to the teacher's discretion. The basic guideline to follow is to enunciate sounds of heard letters within words and help students develop their ability to write a letter for sounds heard. The teacher should call the students' attention to any silent letter(s) that is part of the written word.

Reviews

This module affords time for whole-class instruction as well as reviews during the writing portion of the 30 minutes. Although originally designed as one of the remedial aspects in this program, the phonics reviews are usually met with enthusiasm by all students in the class, since the words in the reviews come from them. There are many words containing whatever letter(s) is being studied. All students should have the opportunity to participate in the search for some of these words. Obviously, the students who need the lessons most should receive them. More advanced students enjoy the challenge of presenting new words containing certain elements. In these reviews, no one should be stereotyped or set apart in a small group from the rest of the class. The range of word offerings during the reviews can be from *egg* to *executive suite.*

HOW TO TEACH THE PHONICS/SPELLING MODULE

There are three major parts of each Phonics/Spelling Module.

Selection of Vocabulary from Students

The teacher writes the alphabet symbol(s) emphasized in the module on a sheet of chart paper taped with masking tape to the chalkboard. Students observe how the symbol(s) is formed. The teacher should say the letter name of the symbol(s) but not assign any other sound to it at this point. The sound will be determined according to its placement in various words.

The teacher then asks students for any words that have the letter(s) in them. As students identify such words, the teacher writes on the chart paper a minimum of twelve words containing the letter(s). Example words containing the letter(s) are included in each module in the appendices; however, these should be used only if the students cannot correctly identify words containing the letter(s) studied.

After each example has been written on the chart paper, the teacher underlines the letter(s) emphasized in the lesson to call the students' attention to it, pronounces the word, and slightly emphasizes the sound of the various letters as they are voiced in each word. The students and teacher can briefly discuss the meaning(s) of each word.

Students should observe the teacher writing *each word* selected in the introductory part of this module. Under no circumstance should the teacher write words on the chalkboard prior to the students' arrival in the classroom.

Students may volunteer words that do not contain the letter symbol(s) emphasized in the lesson. If, for example, the symbol is t and a student volunteers the word *lamp,* the teacher should

1. Move to a part of the chalkboard away from the space where the words containing t have been written.
2. Write the word *lamp* and ask students to note that the spelling of *lamp* does not include a t. (The teacher should not press the point or embarrass the student.)
3. Move back to the part of the board where words containing t are being written and ask for a word containing t.

This part of each Phonics/Spelling Module should last for approximately 15 minutes.

Writing Element in the Phonics/Spelling Process

The remainder of the 30 minutes in this module affords time for the students to practice writing as many of the examples from the chalkboard as possible. Each student should not be expected to write all of the examples. Some students will use the same amount of time to write one word that other students will use to write five or more words. The object is to write letters to make words that can be read; in other words, to improve reading and writing simultaneously, not for each student to write a certain number of words.

The teacher moves from student to student during the writing part of this module. When looking at each student's writing efforts, the teacher should find *something* on the page about which to comment positively. For example, the teacher may compliment the students on how they form a particular letter or letters, the spacing of the letters or words, or improvement in writing their names and the date. Praise can make the difference between motivating students or discouraging them.

During the writing part of this module, the teacher has opportunities to individualize instruction by moving from student to student, commenting positively on the writing abilities of students, and holding the following individualized sessions with students who, in the teacher's opinion, need additional review:

1. The teacher comments positively on *something* students have written prior to the teacher's arrival at their desk.
2. The teacher writes the phonics letter(s) on the student's paper and tells the student the alphabet letter name.
3. The teacher writes on the student's paper two or three words containing the letter(s) as the student observes. These words could be, but perhaps should not be, the same as the ones used in the initial Phonics/Spelling Module for that letter(s).
4. Since the students in need of this review may not be able to write words successfully from the chalkboard, they have a model of words written by the teacher on their paper. The teacher asks the student to practice writing those words, or at least parts of the words.

TABLE 3 Comparison of Phonics

SUCCESS IN BEGINNING READING AND WRITING PHONICS MODULES	PHONICS LESSONS TYPICAL IN SOME OTHER PROGRAMS
1. Vocabulary used in Phonics/Spelling Modules is unlimited in possibilities.	1. Vocabulary used in phonics instruction restricted to examples printed in the lessons.
2. Selection of vocabulary for phonics study is made by students, depending on their word knowledge and understanding.	2. Selection made by adults.
3. Emphasis in phonics instruction is on learning to read a wide variety of words containing the alphabet symbol.	3. Emphasis is on learning a restricted and artificial grouping of words that contain the same phonic sound and alphabet symbol.
4. Emphasis is on learning to read independently words and word clusters, whether the alphabet symbol is in the initial position, final position, or any other part of the word.	4. Emphasis is on learning words with the placement of the alphabet symbol(s) in the same position.
5. Students are taught to read words containing an alphabet symbol, no matter what sound(s) is given to that symbol, even if there is no vocal sound for the symbol.	5. Emphasis is on learning to make sounds appropriate to given symbols in preselected words.
6. No predetermined judgment of difficulty level of words; any word containing the symbol is acceptable, and no attempt is made to include only short, easy words in any lesson.	6. Careful selection of short "easy" words early in the lesson, with possible progression to longer words.
7. Student writing of letters, words, phrases, and stories containing phonic symbol(s) being studied is included in each module.	7. Student writing of phonics elements usually considered secondary; not included at all in some programs.
8. Examples of words and word clusters containing the phonic elements emphasized in each module are heard by the students before, during, and after the students observe the teacher writing the words on the chalkboard.	8. Examples are already printed, and students do not observe the process of developing the letters in sequence to make the words.
9. Selected examples of the words studied are placed on charts and hung in the classroom for the remainder of the school year for reviews, reference for spelling, and as a visual record of some word(s) studied by this class.	9. No long-term phonics reference points in the classroom.
10. No two classes may be alike in their selection of phonics inclusions. Student and teacher differences can be taken into honest and effective consideration.	10. All students follow the same predetermined phonics words to study.
11. All classes follow the same *process* in educating students to use phonic aids when possible in reading *any* word and to realize that phonics is not helpful in pronouncing some words.	11. The process of using phonics clues is secondary to the motions of becoming familiar with blends, digraphs, long and short vowel sounds, etc.
12. Phonics rules are never taught; however, some students can make their own generalizations.	12. Phonics rules (*i* before *e* except after *c*, etc.) stressed in some programs.
13. Because of the built-in freedom in selectivity of words to study from pronunciation as well as meaning, this program provides ample study opportunity for the developmentally delayed students in the class as well as the academically talented and other students between the two extremes. For example, the first module could contain the words *ball* and *benzaldehyde*—if students volunteered those words.	13. Phonics taught on a track system, highly controlled from easy to more difficult words in a time sequence.

5. The teacher probably will not be able to work individually every day with each student in need of review. It is better to help a few individuals in the manner described above, and additional students on following days, than to try to reach a number of these students in an artifically contrived small-group situation.

Dating and Filing Student Papers

At the end of the Phonics/Spelling Module, the students' papers should be dated and filed in folders placed alphabetically in a box labeled *Phonics/Spelling*. The chart developed in the module should be hung in the classroom.

ADDITIONAL READING

Adams, Anne H. *Sounds For Me*. San Francisco: Leswing Communications, Inc., 1971.

Heilman, Arthur W. *Phonics in Proper Perspective*. Columbus, Ohio: Charles E. Merrill Publishing Company, 1976.

Henderson, Ellen C. *Phonics in Learning to Read: A Handbook for Teachers*. New York: Exposition Press, Inc., 1967.

Hull, Marion A. *Phonics for the Teacher of Reading*. Columbus, Ohio: Charles E. Merrill Publishing Company, 1976.

Schell, Robert E. *Letters and Sounds, A Manual for Reading Instruction*. Englewood Cliffs, N.J.: Prentice-Hall, Inc., 1972.

BACKGROUND INFORMATION CONCERNING PHONICS IN THIS PROGRAM

In this program, phonics elements are defined as emphasis on the following individual letter or letter combinations (clusters): 26 small letters, 26 capital letters, 40 letter clusters, plus 84 letters or letter clusters with particular emphasis on syllabication. Phonics is *one* aspect of reading instruction. This program presents ways to improve phonics instruction—to make it more meaningful to all students as well as to make it a more productive tool in both reading and writing. Table 3 shows some of the phonics instruction improvements in this program compared with phonics treatment in other programs.

chapter four
The Language Experience Module

PURPOSE

The major purpose of the Language Experience Modules is to correlate student writing, speaking, listening, and reading. Each day, beginning with the first day of the first grade, students should get help in writing and reading letters, words, word clusters, sentences, paragraphs, and/or stories related to each one's unique experiences. The Language Experience Module affords time for students to build writing and reading skills on understandings they have and would like to share with others.

SCHEDULING

The 174 suggested language experience activities in this program are found in Appendices One through Four. Table 4 shows the language experience emphasis for each lesson.

Each theme can be developed over a three-day cycle (three 30-minute modules), if that amount of time is needed for the students to complete their writing. However, composition types and themes other than those indicated for the first ninety modules can be added at the teacher's discretion and according to immediate interests of the students. For example, if it snows unexpectedly one day, the students might write about it rather than the designated theme for that day.

GUIDELINES FOR CONTENT SELECTION

Each Language Experience Module must include talking, listening, writing, reading what one has written, and filing that writing in each student's folder in the box labeled *Language Experience. The date should be recorded on each paper.* These papers are not sent home until the end of the year.

Themes

Phases 1–3 identify themes for development in each Language Experience Module. The themes are based on topics all students can identify with and have something to say and write about. Teachers may

TABLE 4   Suggested Language Experience Plan

LESSON	THEMES AND TOPICS	LESSON	THEMES AND TOPICS
1–15	Self (subtopics: things I like, things I do, things I see, things I hear, things I feel)	120–121	Writing story; no theme
		122–123	Writing friendly letters
16–33	Environment (subtopics: animals, people, birds, houses, furniture, toys)	124–125	Writing story; no theme
		126–127	Writing business letters
34–48	Food (subtopics: breakfast, lunch, dinner, taste, colors)	128–130	Writing story; no theme
		131–132	Writing list of items
49–63	Animals (subtopics: dogs, cats, horses, cows, goats)	133–134	Writing story
		135–137	Writing poem
64–66	Cartoons	138–140	Writing story
67–69	Television programs (subtopics: not a cartoon, happy, news)	141–143	Writing poem
		144–145	Writing story
70–72	People at school	146–148	Writing poem
73–75	Places at school	149–151	Writing story
76–78	Places to go	152–153	Writing poem
79–81	Games	154–155	Writing story
82–84	Toys	156–157	Writing factual information
85–87	Clothes	158–159	Writing story
88–90	School	160–162	Writing factual information
91–111	Story writing; no theme	163–165	Writing story
112–113	Writing friendly letters	166–167	Writing factual information
114–115	Writing memos	168–170	Writing story
116–117	Story writing; no theme	171–172	Writing factual information
118–119	Writing business letters	173–174	Writing story

wish to add additional themes; however, the following ten global themes should be considered as the minimum:

1. Self
2. Pictures
3. Food
4. Animals
5. Toys
6. Television
7. Play
8. Travel
9. Clothes
10. School

Many themes have five suggested subtopics, intended to provide assistance to students in developing specific ideas about the theme. For example, *Things I Like* is the first subtopic. The students are asked to tell things they like, and the teacher writes some of these items, such as *horses, peanut butter, television, trucks,* and *blue* on the chalkboard *as the students observe the writing of the words.* These words should remain on the board for the rest of that module; however, each child should not be expected to include all of the words in his or her composition.

The idea is to identify themes and subthemes for each day's Language Experience Module, especially during the first half of the academic year. Beginning with Lesson 91, many lessons encourage students to write about any theme they wish to develop in writing. In the latter part of the year, specific time is also allocated for students to write things other than stories (see Chapter Eight).

In the three days of thematic development, at least one word volunteered by *each* student in the class should be among those written on the chalkboard. The same students should not dominate this portion of the program. The teacher and students should discuss at least one meaning of each word or cluster listed.

The stories do not have to be finished on the first day of that theme. One objective is to show students that writers do not finish all their work at one sitting. There is no objection to writing portions on one day and additions on other days. Learning to budget work times and finding a safe place to keep the work until it can be resumed are essential study skills that should be initiated even in the first grade.

Student-Created Compositions

Regardless of its length, each language experience writing should be called a "story" and should be dated and filed in the student's folder.

Every child in the class should write stories. Even if the definition of "story" is so loosely interpreted as to mean the formation of a partial letter, a letter, or a word, one of the most important aspects a teacher can accomplish is to help people (as young as age six) realize they can express themselves in writing and that what they have to say can be meaningful to other people. At this stage, efforts in written expression rather than emphasis on correctness of form or spelling should be encouraged. *Praise is more important than criticism.*

Motivation to write stories and other forms of written communication is provided primarily through teacher praise concerning some aspect of the student's work, followed by a constructive suggestion for improvement, such as the addition of another word to add dimension to a character's description. The two ingredients—*positive reinforcement* concerning what has been written by the student and *constructive suggestion* concerning an item that might be changed—are essential parts of the teacher's role in this part of the program.

During the first half of the first grade, language experience papers should not be marked where errors occur in grammar and spelling. Such markings should begin during the latter part of the year, unless individual students have enough knowledge of these aspects of written language that teacher-made corrections will be helpful to the student. Excessive correction of errors before students have sufficient background will hinder rather than help them. Under no circumstance does this program advocate teaching students that they cannot do things correctly. Therefore, such comments as "You've started a good story" or "I think your character, Lucy, has good possibilities" are more appropriate than "You left out periods," or "You misspelled gost (ghost)." One of the teacher's jobs is to convince students that they *can* achieve in reading and writing.

Beginning with Phase 4 (Lesson 91) proofreading is emphasized for each subtheme's composition(s). Proofreading may be done by the student on his or her own paper under the teacher's direction, by two students checking each other's papers, or by small peer groups discussing and evaluating the papers of their members. Proofreading should be limited, with individual exceptions, to the single emphasis included in the lessons for two reasons. First, the students (or groups) will understand the assignment better and be more thorough, since their attention is directed toward a single task. Second, the corrections made on the papers will not be so numerous that students will become discouraged about their writing ability.

Individual writing skills improve as the teacher moves among the students while they are writing and helps one student capitalize the first letter in a sentence, helps another student insert an adjective to improve a description, shows another student the need for a period, and helps another student turn a phrase into a sentence. This approach seems to be more meaningful to students than having whole-class instruction on a particular writing skill that may or may not be understood by all students. Instead, if the teacher calls attention to a particular item on a student's paper, there is a greater chance that the student will immediately grasp its implications.

Students who learn to form letters into words are on the way to putting those words into phrases, the phrases into sentences, sentences into paragraphs, and the paragraphs into different kinds of stories. This 30-minute period per day is devoted to helping students move from rudimentary pencil scratching to the writing of rather complicated stories. Such an objective is worth at least 30 minutes of each day.

Writing Resources in the Classroom

A built-in component in this program is an emphasis on students locating and correcting their own errors. Because the language experience writings are saved in a folder for the entire year, students can look back at their earlier writing and discern any errors.

The phonics/spelling and patterning charts hanging in the classroom give students a rich spelling resource. Under no circumstances should the charts be omitted from the program. Each chart should be displayed so that students can see all the items.

Dictionaries are extremely helpful to students in this module.

HOW TO TEACH THE LANGUAGE EXPERIENCE MODULE

There are four parts of each composition developed over a three-day period during Language Experience Modules.

Introduction of Writing Theme (day one of theme development)

The teacher writes the theme (*Self,* for example) on the chalkboard. Students and teacher talk for a few minutes about its various meanings and implications. The teacher then leads the discussion to focus on a subtopic. For example, one of the *Self* subtopics is *Things I Like.*

Students then volunteer key vocabulary words about the particular subtopic, and the teacher writes them on the chalkboard while the students watch. In this part of the lesson, there is an integral correlation of listening, speaking, reading, writing, and spelling.

After some words or word clusters have been written, the teacher conducts a quick review of each word or cluster by pointing to it and asking the class to read it in unison.

This part of the module should take approximately 10 minutes.

Student Creative Writing (day one of theme development)

Using the theme, the students begin writing a story, poem, letter, etc. for the remainder of the module time. They may or may not use the words on the chalkboard; however, the words serve as a resource for students who need them.

Students determine a "stopping place" in time for the writing to be filed in their folders before the end of the 30 minutes.

Expansion of Creative Writing (day two of theme development)

The teacher returns the previous day's papers to the students. They continue the discussion concerning the theme and subtheme. The teacher writes key words associated with the theme on the chalkboard. However, these words should be different from the words introduced on the previous day.

Students reread what they wrote the day before.

For the rest of the 30-minute period students can continue their previous day's writing or begin writing something else on the same or a different subject.

During the student composition time on both days, the teacher helps individual students at their desks. In addition, the teacher may write other key words related to the theme on the chalkboard to help students with ideas for additions to their writing.

The papers are dated and filed in the students' folders.

Proofreading and Polishing the Composition (day three of theme development)

The students finish their writing.

During Phases 1–3, students reread their own completed papers for omitted words, grammatical errors, and misspelled words.

Beginning with Phase 4, proofreading for specific types of error becomes part of each two-day writing cycle. Proofreading is included in the lessons of Phase 4. Suggestions for proofreading include:

1. Explaining the proofreading concept through group discussion and examples written on the chalkboard. Students then proofread their own papers.
2. Making a transparency of a student's paper. The entire class proofreads this paper. Each student then proofreads his or her own paper.
3. Students working in pairs to proofread each other's papers.
4. Students working in small groups (three to four students). Each person reads his or her own paper and the others assist in evaluating it for the proofreading skill emphasized.

Other activities that might be included on the third day are:

1. Illustrating the writing (student art work and photographs should be included frequently in this module; however, any art work *must* be accompanied by student writing).
2. Reading the story, poem, etc. to others in the class.
3. Writing a note to parents describing the composition.

The papers are dated and filed in student folders.

ADDITIONAL READING

Aukerman, Robert C. *Approaches to Beginning Reading.* New York: John Wiley and Sons, Inc., 1971. See especially Chapter 7.

Hall, Mary Anne. *Teaching Reading as a Language Experience.* Columbus, Ohio: Charles E. Merrill Publishing Company, 1976.

Lee, Dorris M., and VanAllen, R. *Learning to Read through Experience.* New York: Appleton-Century-Crofts, 1963.

Stauffer, Russell G. *The Language Experience Approach to the Teaching of Reading.* New York: Harper & Row Publishers, 1970.

_____. *Teaching Reading as a Thinking Process.* New York: Harper & Row Publishers, 1969. See especially Chapter 8.

chapter five
The Academic, Cultural Arts, and Current Events Reading Module

PURPOSE

Television and word-of-mouth communications must not be people's only information resources. A literate, informed society should be able to use textbooks, newspapers, magazines, and many other forms of printed materials. The first grade is a good place to begin this process.

The concept of learning to read as developed in this program encompasses introducing students to a wealth of knowledge found in a variety of printed sources. To accomplish this, the teaching of specific reading skills and themes are incorporated within modules where the students use books and other materials of the type they will encounter in the future. In this manner, reading skills are not taught in settings isolated from the mainstream of science, mathematics, social studies, art, music, and current events information in print.

First graders can become engrossed in content and pictures of textbooks written for older students. One major purpose of using science, social studies, and mathematics textbooks from grades beyond first grade is to introduce students to academic-type reading styles. The objective is not to require students to learn specific content in the books. The purpose is to provide students with opportunities to begin to develop a familiarity and identification with such books.

By the end of the year, students should have developed the habit of reading the newspaper, become familiar with the kinds of information available in various popular magazines, be aware that textbooks are a delightful source of information, and realize the assortment of printed information on labels, maps, forms, and so on.

SCHEDULING

To develop this part of this program, there are fifty-two modules based on reading textbooks, forty-eight modules based on reading newspapers, and forty-eight modules based on reading magazines. There are also seven modules for reading catalogues, seven for telephone books, seven map-reading activities, and five activities involving forms. Table 5 shows the kinds of module teaching emphases. Ideas for each module are presented in more detail in Appendices One through Four.

TABLE 5 Suggested Reading for Information Plan

LESSON	MATERIAL	TOPIC/THEME	LESSON	MATERIAL	TOPIC/THEME
1—2	Newspaper	b, c	65—66	Social studies textbook	important words in chapter titles
3—4	Magazine	food	67	Newspaper	E, e
5—6	Science textbook	main idea	68	Newspaper	I, i
7	Newspaper	d	69—70	Magazine	children
8	Newspaper	f	71—72	Math textbook	words for objects
9—10	Magazine	hands	73	Newspaper	O, o
11—12	Social studies textbook	sequence of events	74	Newspaper	U, u
13	Newspaper	G, g	75—76	Magazine	cars
14	Newspaper	H, h	77—78	Science textbook	words that describe
15—16	Magazine	eyes	79—80	Newspaper	sight words
17—18	Math textbook	direction words	81—82	Magazine	pictures and words with the *r* sound
19	Newspaper	J, j	83—84	Social studies textbook	index
20	Newspaper	K, k			
21—22	Magazine	feet	85—86	Newspaper	*TV Guide*
23—24	Science textbook	-ing	87—88	Magazine	*d* sound
25	Newspaper	L, l	89—90	Math textbook	symbols
26	Newspaper	M, m	91—92	Newspaper	photograph captions
27—28	Magazine	television	93—94	Newspaper	sports story
29—30	Social studies textbook	words ending in *ed*	95	Catalogue	toy advertisements
31	Newspaper	N, n	96	Newspaper	front page news story
32	Newspaper	P, p	97	Newspaper	photograph captions
33—34	Magazine	money	98	Newspaper	front page news story
35—36	Math textbook	specialized words	99	Catalogue	furniture advertisements
37	Newspaper	Q, q	100	Newspaper	state news
38	Newspaper	R, r	101	Newspaper	sports story
39—40	Magazine	water	102	Catalogue	clothing advertisements
41—42	Science textbook	specialized words	103	Newspaper	classified ads: miscellaneous
43	Newspaper	S, s	104	Newspaper	news story of local interest
44	Newspaper	T, t	105	Newspaper	information about television programs
45—46	Magazine	birds	106	Catalogue	appliance advertisements
47—48	Social studies textbook	items in pictures	107	Newspaper	front page news story
49	Newspaper	V, v	108	Newspaper	news story of local interest
50	Newspaper	W, w	109	Newspaper	classified ads: pets
51—52	Magazine	airplanes	110	Catalogue	toy advertisements
53—54	Math textbook	words for places			
55	Newspaper	X, x			
56	Newspaper	Y, y			
57—58	Magazine	hair			
59—60	Science textbook	words referring to people			
61	Newspaper	Z, z			
62	Newspaper	A, a			
63	Magazine	toys			
64	Magazine	feelings			

TABLE 5   (*continued*)

LESSON	MATERIAL	TOPIC/THEME	LESSON	MATERIAL	TOPIC/THEME
111	Newspaper	information about television programs	143	Social studies textbook	using context clues
112–113	Magazine	reading a story	144	Map reading	rivers
114	Telephone book	yellow pages: groceries	145	Social studies textbook	locating descriptive words
115	Magazine	reading advertisements	146	Math textbook	locating important facts
116	Magazine	reading a story	147	Map reading	streets
117	Magazine	reading advertisements	148	Math textbook	locating descriptive words
118	Magazine	completing forms	149	Science textbook	locating important facts
119	Telephone book	yellow pages: automobiles	150	Science textbook	reading to draw conclusions
120–122	Magazine	reading a story	151	Social studies textbook	locating important facts
123	Telephone book	yellow pages: appliances	152	Map reading	landmarks
124–125	Magazine	reading advertisements	153	Math textbook	specialized vocabulary
126	Magazine	reading a story	154	Newspaper	news story
127	Telephone book	white pages: locating numbers	155	Magazine	reading a story
128	Magazine	reading a story	156	Form	completing forms
129	Magazine	reading advertisements	157	Catalogue	make a mock order
130	Telephone book	white pages: locating numbers	158	Telephone book	locating numbers
131	Magazine	reading advertisements	159	Map	highways
132	Magazine	reading a story	160	Form	completing forms
133	Science textbook	reading for main ideas	161	Science textbook	locating causes and effects
134	Science textbook	locating direction words	162	Social studies textbook	locating causes and effects
135	Social studies textbook	reading for main ideas	163	Math textbook	following directions
136	Map reading	streets	164	Newspaper	news story
137	Social studies textbook	locating direction words	165	Form	completing forms
138	Math textbook	locating direction words	166	Magazine	table of contents
139	Math textbook	locating details in problems	167	Catalogue	index
140	Map reading	landmarks	168	Telephone book	yellow pages: schools
141	Science textbook	using context clues	169	Form	completing forms
142	Science textbook	locating descriptive words	170	Map	planning a trip
			171	Science textbook	specialized vocabulary
			172	Social studies textbook	specialized vocabulary
			173	Form	completing forms
			174	Newspaper	news story

Each activity emphasizing the use of the three major kinds of printed materials used in this module —*textbooks, newspapers,* and *magazines*—can be scheduled for two consecutive days during Phases 1–3. A cycle can be completed in six days. For example:

Monday and Tuesday—reading instruction using newspapers

Wednesday and Thursday—reading instruction using magazines

Friday and Monday—reading instruction using textbooks

Tuesday and Wednesday—reading instruction using newspapers

In addition, the teacher is encouraged to incorporate other materials, such as catalogues, forms, letters, maps, telephone books, and boxes containing printed information into this 30-minute component along with part of the textbook, magazine, and newspaper lessons.

GUIDELINES FOR CONTENT SELECTION

Use of Newspapers and Magazines

There are major differences between the magazine and newspaper activities. Whereas the newspaper activities provide review and extension of phonics and other specific reading skills, the magazine activities are organized around themes to review as well as to expand the theme approach used in many of the Language Experience Modules. The themes, however, are not the same in both modules.

The teacher should help students locate magazines and newspapers, paste, and file their work. As soon as possible, the teacher should encourage students to write explanatory or interpretative words, phrases, sentences, and eventually paragraphs on the paper containing items they have pasted. Although elements of student reaction and interpretation of newspaper and magazine items are certainly not ignored early in the year, articles and stories are emphasized to a greater extent toward the end of the year.

Cardboard boxes placed around the classroom are helpful for holding the newspapers and magazines. Paste, paper, and pencils are needed for the newspaper and magazine lessons, and scissors are optional.

Use of Textbooks, Grades One–Six

Mathematics, social studies, and science are the three major textbook areas used in these modules. Basal and supplementary readers are considered books of "short stories" and are not considered as content-area textbooks.

In each textbook-based lesson, the reading emphasis is on the development of specific reading study skills through association with content. For example, an assignment would be to locate signal words, such as *first, instead of,* or *before,* that offer specific information within an explanation. That kind of assignment should be made in the content-area activity in which the ability to detect signal words will help the student interpret the specialized information.

Since most first grades do not have these kinds of textbooks, arrangements should be made to get second- through sixth-grade level textbooks in the first-grade classrooms. One place to begin the search is in the book storage room.

The basic pattern of instruction emphasis for the various materials during the first half of the year is:

application of phonics skills: newspapers
developing knowledge about themes: magazines
application of comprehension reading skills: textbooks

HOW TO TEACH THE ACADEMIC, CULTURAL ARTS, AND CURRENT EVENTS READING MODULE

There are two basic parts to each Academic, Cultural Arts, and Current Events Reading Module even though the types of reading material used may differ.

Introduction of Reading Skill or Theme Focus

Refer to the module suggestions in the appendices for the type of material and reading skill or theme focus.

Provide individual or small groups of students with copies of the material (newspapers, textbooks, forms, etc.) designated for the module.

Many students will need help initially in unfolding and folding newspapers, in detecting the different sections, and in gross observation of different parts, such as articles and different-sized advertisements. Students may need help in learning the various parts of magazines, such as stories, table of contents, advertisements, and so on. In textbooks, students may need help in locating chapter divisions, subheadings, picture captions, and various other elements.

Write on the chalkboard and discuss examples of the module's theme and/or designated reading skill emphasis.

Ask students to locate at least one word or picture example of the skill or theme in the material. For example:

In Lesson 1–2, students find the letters b and c in words in newspapers.

In Lessons 3–4, students find pictures and/or words associated with a food theme.

In Lessons 5–6, students find a main idea of anything (picture, word, chapter title, caption, sentence, etc.) in a science textbook.

In Lesson 159, students locate any highway on a road map.

This part of the module should take approximately 10 minutes.

Student Application of Reading Skill or Theme to a Specific Material

For the remainder of the module time, the students use the materials in the following manner:

Newspapers

1. Locate certain letters and words in the newspaper.
2. Cut or tear the items selected.
3. Paste the items on paper.
4. Discuss the sound(s) and/or meaning(s) of the items.
5. Date and file the paper containing the items in a folder placed alphabetically in a box labeled *Magazine and Newspaper Reading.*

Magazines

1. Locate in magazines item(s) such as pictures, words, phrases, paragraphs, articles, advertisements, etc.
2. Associate items found with the module's theme.
3. Remove the item(s) from the magazine and paste it on paper.
4. Write on the paper additional letters and/or words related to the theme.
5. Date the paper and file it in the student's folder in a box labeled *Magazine and Newspaper Reading.*

Content area textbooks

1. Help students locate examples in the textbooks. There is little student writing on days the content area textbooks are used.
2. Time should be spent by students in searching for information in print and in sharing information found with other students.

ADDITIONAL READING

Adams, Anne H.; Coble, Charles R.; and Hounshell, Paul B. *Mainstreaming Language Arts and Social Studies: Special Ideas and Activities for the Whole Class.* Santa Monica, Calif.: Goodyear Publishing Co., Inc., 1977.

Coble, Charles R.; Hounshell, Paul B.; and Adams, Anne H. *Mainstreaming Science and Mathematics: Special Ideas and Activities for the Whole Class.* Santa Monica, Calif.: Goodyear Publishing Co., Inc., 1977.

chapter six
The Patterning Module

PURPOSE

The Patterning Module affords emphasis on (1) identical *letter combination patterns* in initial, medial, or final positions in different words, and on (2) recognizing shades of meaning caused by different voice patterns of *stress, pitch,* and *junctures* during oral reading. An example of the first emphasis is found in the cluster family pattern in words such as *stray, str*atosphere, *str*ucture, and *str*eet.

Greater *stress* or intensity placed on words changes the meaning of the sentence:

Did *you* eat that apple?
Did you eat *that* apple?

Meaning can also be affected by the raising or lowering of voice level, or *pitch*, when pronouncing certain words within a sentence:

Did you *eat* that apple? (voice becomes high, shrill)
Did you *eat* that apple? (voice is lowered to a whisper)

Junctures are pauses in sentences that completely change the meaning:

Did you eat that . . . apple?
Did . . . you eat that apple?

The Patterning Module can be used effectively with all students from the reading delayed to the gifted readers in the class.

For students in need of extra help, the Patterning Modules offer a built-in remedial program rather than an approach that does not relate directly to the student's program of study. Students who do not readily understand the Phonics/Spelling Module have a powerful second chance to succeed with the cluster-patterns approach to decoding words. Both the phonics activities in which the letter appears in various places within words and the patterning approach that uses the repetition of internal word features are necessary components in a balanced reading program. For students in the initial stages of learning to read and write, words in the Patterning Module might include:

bat
format
fat
trap
treat
trip

For students who have moved beyond the first stages in learning to read and write, the patterning lessons afford a flexible base for developing advanced vocabularies containing some identical sound elements. For example, these advanced students might learn the pronunciation, meaning(s), and spelling of words such as:

trillion
trillium
trilogy

SCHEDULING

Patterning Modules are taught during the first half of the year in Lessons 1–90. There are 113 sound symbols emphasized in these modules. Beginning with Lesson 91, the 30-minute Patterning Module is deleted; however, its basic components of cluster patterns, stress, pitch, and juncture should be included spontaneously as the need for them arises during the second half of the year.

Table 6 illustrates the sequence of the patterns. Additional information for each Patterning Module is in Appendices One through Three.

GUIDELINES FOR CONTENT SELECTION

In each Patterning Module, reading should be correlated with use of the words in different vocal settings. Among the most specific components in the Patterning Modules are:

1. Student suggestions of words with the same patterns (hat, cat, fat; photograph, photolens, telephoto).
2. Student use of different vocal stresses in phrases and sentences.
3. Student use of different vocal pitches in phrases and sentences.
4. Student use of different junctures in phrases and sentences.
5. Student creation of instuctional materials.

Each of the five should be included in each Patterning Module.

Student Selection of Words Containing the Same Pattern in the Same Position

In the Patterning Module, the position, as well as the selection of words containing the letter(s) being studied, is extremely important. This approach is different from the Phonics/Spelling Module in which the only stipulation is that the letter(s) being studied is found in the words presented, and the position of the letter(s) in the words does not matter. Part of each day's lesson should afford students opportunities to decode words containing similar elements in the same position within words as one aspect of detecting language patterns while improving reading and writing abilities (Patterning). A part of each day's lesson should encourage students to decode words containing the letter(s) in any position (Phonics/Spelling).

The teacher should never impose limitations concerning length of word or apparent ease or difficulty of word pronunciation or meaning. Students should volunteer words containing the cluster pattern emphasized in the module. The teacher writes them on chart paper, which is displayed in the classroom for the remainder of the year.

There probably will be occasions when the discussion of words containing the pattern identified in a module leads to words containing a different pattern. For example, in a module pattern of ba, the students developed words ending in the at pattern from the word bat.

TABLE 6   Suggested Patterning Plan*

LESSON	EMPHASIS	LESSON	EMPHASIS	LESSON	EMPHASIS	LESSON	EMPHASIS
1	bă	24	hĭ	47	pē	69	er, ir, ur
2	bĕ	25	hŏ	48	pī	70	er, ir ,ur
3	bĭ	26	hŭ	49	pō	71	or
4	bŏ	27	jă	50	wā	72	dy
5	bŭ	28	jĕ, jĭ	51	rē	73	oo, ew
6	că	29	jŏ	52	rī	74	ss
7	cŏ	30	jŭ	53	rō	75	oi, oy
8	cŭ	31	kĕ	54	rū, sū	76	ll
9	dă	32	kĭ	55	sā	77	al, all
10	dĕ	33	lă	56	sē	78	au, aw
11	dĭ	34	lĕ	57	sī, sō	79	un
12	dŏ	35	lĭ	58	tā	80	oo, u
13	dŭ	36	lŏ, lŭ	59	tē	81	ble
14	fă	37	mă	60	tī	82	ou, ow
15	fĕ	38	mĕ	61	tŏ, tŭ	83	pp
16	fĭ	39	mĭ	62	vā, vē	84	en, ed
17	fŏ	40	mŏ	63	vī, vō	85	ar
18	fŭ	41	mŭ	64	wā	86	gn, kn
19	gă	42	nă	65	wē	87	mp
20	gŏ	43	nĕ	66	wī	88	ly
21	gŭ	44	nĭ	67	wŏ, yŏ	89	n't
22	hă	45	nŏ, nŭ	68	yē, zē	90	tion, sion
23	hĕ	46	pā				

*The Patterning Module is deleted after Lesson 90.

bat ⟶ cat
band   rat
basket   sat

As soon as possible in the year, each student should be encouraged to volunteer words containing identical letter clusters other than those placed on the chalkboard and to use those words in developing poems, tongue twisters, puzzles, stories, and the like.

The Effect of Voice on Reading Comprehension

The teacher should ask students to read words, phrases, and/or sentences aloud using different stress, pitch, and juncture to help them understand the impact made on meanings and interpretations given to the words.

Student Creation of Instructional Materials

Development of manipulative objects and/or art activities are an important aspect of *each* Patterning Module; however, these items should be created by the *students*, rather than by the teacher. To make the item, the students follow direction guides given by the teacher. Then the students write on the object examples containing the clusters emphasized in the module.

Suggestions for a different manipulative object or art activity for each of the 90 Patterning Modules are found in Appendices One through Three.

HOW TO TEACH THE PATTERNING MODULE

Selection of Vocabulary Containing Pattern Clusters

During the first part of each Patterning Module, the teacher writes and pronounces the cluster(s) emphasized in the module on chart paper taped to the chalkboard. The chart is displayed in the classroom for students' future reference.

There is no student writing of these words during the first part of each Patterning Module.

Beginning with Lesson 11, clusters of words should be included on the patterning charts, such as:

don't drop the drum
the big fig

As students volunteer words containing those letters (and where indicated, certain sounds of letters), the teacher writes the words on the chalkboard. See Charts 8 and 9 in Chapter Two.

Stress, Pitch, and Juncture Emphases

The teacher should use the words orally in sentences indicating different stress, pitch, and juncture. For example, if one of the words is *apple*, students verbally add other words to make a sentence containing the word *apple*. Emphasis is on using different stress, pitch, and juncture while using the sentence in different ways.

A suggested stress, pitch, or juncture guide is in each Patterning Module in the appendices and is presented in the following manner over a twelve-day cycle:

Stress emphasis

1. Vocal stress on one word near the beginning of sentences.
2. Vocal stress on one word in the middle of sentences.
3. Vocal stress on one word near the end sentences.

Pitch emphasis

4. Raising voice near beginning of sentences.
5. Raising voice in middle part of sentences.
6. Raising voice near final part of sentences.
7. Lowering voice near beginning of sentences.
8. Lowering voice in middle of sentences.
9. Lowering voice near end of sentences.

Juncture emphasis

10. Pause near beginning of sentences.
11. Pause in middle of sentences.
12. Pause near end of sentences.

The selection of word patterns and inclusion of stress, pitch, or juncture should take approximately 10 minutes of the module.

Creation of Manipulative Objects

During the remainder of the module, each student works with one or two other students in creating an instructional material out of paper, pasteboard, construction paper, and so on.

The teacher draws an example of the game item on the chalkboard and moves between groups of students, giving help when it is needed.

By the end of the 30 minutes, the students write examples showing the cluster pattern on the manipulative device they have created, and read the examples using different stress, pitch, and/or juncture.

Some of the objects have movable parts, and others suggested involve art activities for students. If possible, students should use construction paper to draw and cut out their versions of items.

ADDITIONAL READING

Bloomfield, Leonard, and Barnhart, Clarence L. *Let's Read: A Language Approach.* Detroit: Wayne State University Press, 1961.

Fries, Charles C. *Linguistics and Reading.* New York: Holt, Rinehart and Winston, 1963.

Lamb, Pose. *Linguistics in Proper Perspective.* Columbus, Ohio: Charles E. Merrill Publishing Company, 1977.

Lefevre, Carl A. *Linguistics and the Teaching of Reading.* New York: McGraw-Hill Book Co., Inc., 1964.

Smith, Frank. *Psycholinguistics and Reading.* New York: Holt, Rinehart and Winston, 1973.

The Recreational Reading Module

PURPOSE

Many people do not voluntarily read books. One of the challenges of today's educator is to find ways to change education, to stimulate people's desire to read books.

This program requires a minimum of 30 minutes each day during the first half of the academic year and one hour each day during the remainder of the year for each student to devote to reading library books. This is the time for students to interact quietly with books of their own. The purpose of the Recreational Reading Module is to establish student reading for enjoyment, as well as for information.

SCHEDULING

The first semester, especially, provides 30 minutes to an hour each day for students to read fiction and non-fiction library books and to receive recognition in the form of teacher praise and recording of the titles they have read. During the latter half of the year, students should be doing more in-depth reading. This kind of scheduling is necessary to provide sufficient time for students to want to read large numbers of different kinds of books. Scheduling time alone, however, is not enough to entice students to read. A planned approach designed to teach the students how to read the books, while motivating them to expand their reading tastes is necessary, and the Recreational Reading Modules in this program are designed to do that.

Table 7 indicates the letter/letter cluster emphasis suggested for Lessons 1–75 to help *individual* students decode words in their library books during the Recreational Reading Module. Lessons 76–90 emphasize different types of words and sentences. These guides represent a minimum requirement and should be supplemented by teachers' judgment of other special help students may need. Conferences continue after Lesson 91; however, there are no guides in the module plans in Appendix Four.

GUIDELINES FOR CONTENT SELECTION

Students must be allowed time in school to apply reading skills to reading library books, to develop the

TABLE 7   Recreational Reading Conference Guide

LESSON	WORDS CONTAINING	LESSON	THEMES
1–3	b	76	words at beginning of sentences
4–6	l		
7–9	d	77	words ending in -*ing* and -*ed*
10–12	m		
13–15	s	78	short words
16–18	g	79	long words
19–21	r	80	names of things
22–24	y	81	name of a young person
25–27	p	82	name of an adult
28–30	f	83	words that describe people
31–33	x or z		
34–36	o	84	words that describe animals
37–39	q		
40–42	w	85	action words
43–45	e	86	happy words
46–48	n	87	sad words
49–51	v	88	words for buildings
52–54	u	89	sentences about a person
55–57	j		
58–60	k	90	sentences about a place
61–63	a	91–174	free reading, teacher–student conferences
64–66	c		(no guides in each lesson)
67–69	i		
70–72	h		
73–75	t		

habit of reading, and to increase their desire to read. It is essential that a supply of fiction and nonfiction books be in the classroom for use in this module.

Before students' arrival on the first day of class, the teacher should make arrangements with the school librarian or public library to have thirty to fifty different kinds of library books in the classroom and to rotate books at least once every two weeks during the year. A guideline for each first-grade child to read or examine is 300 books.

Reading for Enjoyment

During "free-reading," the teacher should not be talking to individuals or groups of students, presenting new information, reviewing items already presented, nor any of the other techniques tradition-ally associated with teaching. The concept of "free-reading" means, in essence, the opportunity for students to read or simply browse through books and comics, *without* having to write or tell reports or answer adult-prompted questions about the content.

Comics should be included in the reading-for-enjoyment category. Some people have not recognized that beyond having an appeal to many children, comics also contain many reading aids. Many people see no "educational" value in having comics in the classroom and may voice objections to their presence. The teacher should be prepared to counter these objections with educationally sound reasons for the comics, such as

1. High interest stories
2. Context clues aided by pictures

3. Different print sizes to aid in reading expressions
4. Easily identified dialogues with characters
5. Repetition-of-words technique
6. Action-oriented stories

Because comics can be used easily in Phonics/ Spelling, Language Experience, and Patterning Modules, they are not identified for use in any specific lesson's module. Instead, the comics are a "free-reading" source for students to read in spare moments. In other words, no emphasis is placed on reading or not reading the comics. They are simply in the classroom, and the students decide whether to read them or other materials.

Basal and supplementary reading textbooks can be included with the reading of library books and comics, since they are considered short story books.

Teaching Without Lecturing

Teachers should not reduce the amount of time allocated per day for library book reading. They must realize that they *are* teaching during this part of the program; however, it is a subtle kind of teaching with powerful implications.

This 30 minutes or hour should be a comparatively quiet time during the day, and silence should be stressed from the beginning. It is not a time for oral reading, listening to records or tapes, discussing story plot with another person, or any other potentially distracting element that might interfere with a person's "getting lost" in a book. It is not a time for any student to ask any question at any time he or she wishes to interrupt. The only exception to the quiet rule is the exchange that takes place between the teacher and an *individual student* during a conference.

Teacher–Student Conferences

The teacher should work on a one-to-one basis with students who need extra help in reading books. Module guides for this built-in remedial part of the program are found in Appendices One through Three.

In the first conferences, the teacher will have to provide more direct assistance to students in locating and in decoding words. Conferences later in the year

should be more student-initiated as individuals build skills and confidence in reading.

Records

A record should be kept of the books previewed or read by each child in the class during this 30-minute or hour module. Credit is given in the form of writing the title of the book, number of pages, date started, and date completed or exchanged for another book written on the student's record sheet. Especially early in the year, students should receive credit for simply looking at the pictures in a book. As the year progresses and the students' abilities increase, they record titles after reading parts of a book. As soon as possible, students receive credit for reading entire books.

A record of titles should be kept for each student. At first, the teacher will have to write the information on the record sheet. As the year progresses, students should be encouraged to do this writing themselves.

Figure 1 shows an example of a student record. Teachers can make stencils of such a chart. By the end of the year, students should have many of these record pages stapled together.

HOW TO TEACH THE RECREATIONAL READING MODULE

Silent Reading in Fiction and Nonfiction Books

At the beginning of the Recreational Reading Module, students select one to three library books and take them to their desks. Teachers should not select the books for students.

Each student begins "reading" a book until the book is finished, until the student decides he or she doesn't like the book and wishes to exchange it for another one, or until there is no more time in this part of the schedule. Exchanging books should be encouraged; no student be made to keep a book he or she is not interested in completing.

FIGURE 1   Individualized Student Library Books Record

Student's Name _____

Title of Library Book	Read All of Book	Read Some of Book	Read These Pages — to —	Date Started	Date Ended

Teacher–Student Conferences

Throughout the Recreational Reading Module, the teacher should work *individually* with a minimum of six children. Assuming there are thirty students in the class and the teacher has short conferences with six students per day, each student in the class should have at least one individualized conference with the teacher each week during the Recreational Reading Module.

During all conferences, discussion should pertain to something in the book and the student's reaction to the book as well as the pronunciation and meaning of some of the words written by the student according to the module assignment. The teacher does not have to "check" each student's reaction to every book read.

An alphabet letter or letter cluster is indicated for each of the first ninety Recreational Reading Modules in Appendices One through Three. Obviously, if students can read the books, there is no need to use this guide; however, the letter(s) guides are included as still another built-in remedial aspect for those students who need help unlocking words in the books.

In Lessons 1–75 (during the individual conferences between student and teacher), the teacher helps the student locate words containing the letter(s) in the library books. The teacher uncovers the word letters with his or her finger while slowly enunciating the word. The process is repeated by the child. As soon as possible, the teacher helps the student pronounce word clusters and, finally, entire sentences containing the letter(s) emphasized in the modules. The teacher should discuss with the student the meaning of the word as it is used in context.

ADDITIONAL READING

Aukerman, Robert C. *Approaches to Beginning Reading*. New York: John Wiley and Sons, Inc., 1971. See especially Chapter 9.

Darrow, Helen F., and Howes, Virgil M. *Approaches to Individualized Reading*. New York: Appleton-Century-Crofts, 1960.

Miel, Alice. *Individualized Reading Practice: Practical Suggestions for Teaching*. New York: Columbia University, Teachers College Press, 1958.

Veatch, Jeannette. *Individualizing Your Reading Program: Self-Selection in Action*. New York: G. P. Putnam's Sons, 1959.

The Expansion Phase: The Second Half of the Year

The preceding chapters describe the basic elements in the program taught in roughly the first half of an academic year. The lesson plans for these ninety days are found in Appendices One through Three. The program is expanded and parts of it eliminated or modified in Lessons 91 through 174 (approximately the second half of the academic year). Emphases for specific Expansion Phase lessons are found in Appendix Four.

GENERAL DIRECTIONS

The 2½-hour teaching time block is continued throughout the Expansion Phase of the program. The predominate reading and writing emphasis is on stories and chapters; however, study of individual sentences and paragraphs is also essential. Words in isolation and word clusters are not emphasized.

Students writing should continue to be dated and filed in appropriate folders and a record of library books read by students should be made daily.

Although the meaning(s) of assigned readings is an essential part of the first ninety lessons, comprehension of various interpretations of the items read should be emphasized to a greater degree during the Expansion Phase.

As in the earlier parts of the program, instruction suggestions are given for each module each day (Appendix Four). Teachers develop these suggestions according to their professional expertise and with careful regard to the individual students in the class. In addition, teachers are encouraged to supplement and enrich the lesson suggestions with their own ideas, which only a professional teacher can provide.

MODIFICATION OF THE PHONICS/SPELLING MODULE

1. Follow the same teaching *procedures* and *methodologies* as recommended for the first ninety lessons.
2. Change the *content* emphasis to syllabication and other forms of structural analysis. Phonics components are identified for each Expansion Phase lesson. The emphasis is placed on the sound(s) within the syllable wherein that phonics component is located. For example, if the phonics component is *n*, an example of a sentence might be:

The <u>Con</u>-sti-tu-<u>tion</u> of the U-<u>nit</u>-ed States is im-por-<u>tant</u>.

3. Follow this framework in the Phonics/Spelling Module:

    Lessons 91–121: at least one two-syllable word in each sentence

    Lessons 122–152: at least one three-syllable word in each sentence

    Lessons 153–168: at least one four-syllable word in each sentence

    Lessons 169–174: at least one five-or-more syllable word in each sentence

MODIFICATION OF THE LANGUAGE EXPERIENCE MODULE

1. Students continue writing stories each week during Lessons 91–174. In addition to the stories, other kinds of writing should definitely be included each week. Appendix Four contains a guide for teachers to use; however, only teachers who know the students in their class can determine if the number of lessons suggested for each kind of writing is appropriate for that class.

2. Beginning with Lesson 91, delete the theme approach. Instead, encourage each individual student to the writing of stories.

3. Beginning with Lesson 112, the students should have class time during the Language Experience Module to do other kinds of writing in addition to the writing of stories. Use the following guide for student writing:

    Lessons 91–111: writing stories; any topic

    Lessons 112–132: writing friendly letters; writing business letters; writing stories

    Lessons 133–153: writing poetry; writing stories

    Lessons 154–174: writing factual information; writing stories

4. Occasionally, provide each student with a blank stencil and ask the students to write their stories directly on the stencils. Make sure each student writes his or her name on the stencil as "author" of the story before copies of the stencil are reproduced. Run enough copies of the stencils for each student in the class to have a copy to read, and use these copies as a part of the reading instruction with emphasis on learning to read handwriting produced by different people. Send one copy home to the student's parents.

MODIFICATION OF THE ACADEMIC, CULTURAL ARTS, AND CURRENT EVENTS READING MODULE

1. Continue using newspapers, magazines, and textbooks as the major kinds of materials to be read during Lessons 91–174.

2. Emphasize reading entire selections, such as news or feature stories, advertisements, chapter divisions, instead of word clusters, sentences, or paragraphs.

3. Beginning with Lesson 95, provide students with other kinds of materials to read. Use the following as a minimum guide:

    reading catalogues—5 days

    reading telephone books—5 days

    reading maps—5 days

    reading different kinds of forms—5 days

    A suggested sequence is found in the Academic, Cultural Arts, and Current Events Reading column in Appendix Four.

4. With the exception of the textbooks, the students should cut or tear out entire stories, advertisements, and so on, from the material to be read and concentrate on reading to locate definite kinds of information. Some of this information should be written on paper attached to the printed material. One of the teacher's major roles during the Expansion Phase in this module is to direct the line of questioning in a way that will afford the students a balance between literal reading and interpretative reading. Use at least one of the following comprehension guides in each module to form questions:

    Who is mentioned, described, or implied in the material?

    Where did something happen?

    Why did something happen, according to information given in the material?

    What occurred as indicated in the material?

How did some specific item happen?
When did something happen?

One comprehension guide is included in each module in Appendix Four.

5. Papers containing the student's written answers as well as a copy of the material read (with the exception of textbook pages) should contain the name of the student and the date the work was completed before the papers are filed in the student's folder.

6. In lessons using textbooks, students should write notes concerning some of the information learned after reading the textbook material assigned by the teacher, according to the question emphasis. This note-taking emphasis is extremely important in the program.

DELETION OF THE PATTERNING MODULE

1. Omit the 30-minute patterning lessons for Lessons 91–174.

2. Include symbol cluster patterns, pitch, stress, and juncture components where applicable in other activities in the program.

MODIFICATION OF THE RECREATIONAL READING MODULE

1. Allocate a *full* hour per day instead of 30 minutes for students to read library books.

2. Beginning with Lesson 91, the class should be relatively quiet during the entire Recreational Reading Module; however, this does not mean the teacher–student individual conferences should stop.

3. There should be no writing by students during the library book reading portion of this hour each day.

4. Conferences should be on a teacher-to-individual-student basis, and there should be two kinds of conferences:

Conferences at which a student tells the teacher about a book he or she has read.

Conferences at which the teacher tells the student about a book the teacher has read.

5. Occasionally, bring a novel to school and read silently with the students for a part of the hour each day. This establishes the model of adults' reading for enjoyment and is extremely important, particularly in cases where children have never seen adults read books for fun.

6. Keep student records of titles of books read.

7. Continue sending library books, textbooks, basal readers (grade levels one through six, depending on the reading abilities of the students), and supplementary readers home at least three times during each week. Students need not know all words before taking a book home. If students can read some content, they should be encouraged to experience other successes in reading.

chapter nine
Educators and Others

TEACHERS

Teachers are charged with expanding the parts of the module in each lesson to the extent that they are meaningful to students in their classes. This means each teacher will bring unique contributions to the teaching of reading and writing. The respect for the integrity and ability of professional teachers to both formulate and implement these meaningful contributions is one of the foundations of this program.

Two models were piloted in preparing this program. One model was based on a single teacher in a self-contained classroom. Although successful, this program model resulted in decreased time afforded to each student for individual help. In the second model, two certified elementary or reading teachers worked together for a half day when this program was taught. The second teacher then worked with another class for the remainder of the day to teach the same 2½-hour lesson. Of the two models, the second is without question the most desirable. There simply is not enough time in the day, nor is it physically possible, for one teacher to devote sufficient time to *each* of twenty to thirty-five first graders to produce the necessary reading/writing results before some students experience feelings of failure.

One of the best investments any state and/or school district can make is to employ extra certified first-grade teachers to work in the classrooms with other first-grade teachers. Since the cost factor is an issue, the following guidelines are recommended to people making budget allocations.

1. One first-grade teacher, preferably a certified reading teacher, should be employed to work with one first-grade classroom teacher in the morning and with another first-grade classroom teacher in the afternoon. This reduces the teacher–pupil ratio by half during reading and writing instruction when both teachers are in a classroom.

2. The second first-grade teacher is assigned by the principal to teach this program in one first-grade classroom each morning for 2½ hours, for example, from 9:00–11:30, and to repeat the lesson in the other first-grade classroom in the afternoon, for example, from 12:00–2:30. Principals must schedule these blocks of time so there are no interruptions, such as art or music classes or recesses. The program's lessons should not be broken up but should be presented in the 2½-hour block. This

means some first graders will receive their reading/ writing lessons in the afternoons, out of the traditionally conceived prime teaching time. In the pilot studies, it did not seem to matter whether the children were taught in the afternoon or in the morning. This means, in essence, that a first grader's prime learning time can fall either in the morning or in the afternoon. When time is allocated according to this program's recommendations, $2\frac{1}{2}$ hours of instruction is not too long for first graders. In some classes in the pilot study, the students wished to go beyond the $2\frac{1}{2}$-hour block.

3. All teachers should be certified as teachers. For psychological as well as accountability reasons it is extremely important that the teachers feel qualified to implement and develop the program, for both instruction and explanation to parents.

4. The certified teachers should have completed successfully at least two college or university courses on theories and practices of teaching reading. Such a background gives the teachers a professional perspective to begin teaching the program immediately and, hopefully, enough security to avoid including content or materials that are irrelevant, even if the materials look good.

5. Both teachers assigned to work together must do everything possible to establish an atmosphere of cooperation. It is essential that both understand that the class is the responsibility of two teachers for $2\frac{1}{2}$ hours each day, and neither teacher outranks the other during that time. The objective is to work together—not to get caught up in petty personality problems. When such problems arise the ones who suffer are the students. At the first indications of trouble, both teachers should try to work out the problems. Professional teachers should have the ability and commitment to teach this program. Personal characteristics should not be allowed to thwart it.

6. Whether working alone in the classroom or teamed with another teacher, a teacher should use the key components in each lesson in the program as a guide and should add to each of those components according to his or her expertise.

7. During instruction time other than the 5 hours assigned to work with two first-grade teachers in teaching this program, the additional first-grade teachers should work on a one-to-one tutorial basis with students who need extra help. That teacher should be assigned to alternate on a daily basis between the two classes.

8. To teach this program, the teachers must work; however, the *results make the extra efforts worthwhile*. Teachers *cannot* sit behind their desks and achieve success with their students.

9. The use of untrained or partially trained aides or volunteers should be in addition to the employment of the two teachers. Assignments for aides and volunteers should be made by the teachers; first, to assist in clerical-type duties, such as filing and recording information, and second, to reinforce a particular lesson aspect. To avoid misunderstandings as well as misrepresentation, the differences between the responsibilities of the teachers and the aides and volunteers should be clearly drawn.

ADMINISTRATORS

The first role of the principal is to become familiar with the program in order to understand the underlying theories, to initiate necessary arrangements for implementing the program in the school, and to gain information necessary to discuss the program.

As they read this book, principals should make marginal notes concerning areas that involve action they will take. *Some* of these actions are:

1. Schedule the $2\frac{1}{2}$-hour instructional block. (The block can be broken between modules only.)

2. Locate upper-level content area and reading textbooks and assign those books to the first-grade classes.

3. Meet with the school or public librarian to provide the additional library books in the first-grade classrooms.

4. Order the basic materials needed in the program.

Principals must also disseminate information about the ongoing program in the school.

1. Discuss the role of the two teachers in classroom and make sure the teachers understand that both are equally responsible for teaching.
2. Visit the classes frequently during the 2½-hour block and make sure that each module is being taught.
3. Schedule periodic meetings for the teachers to share ideas concerning techniques each has found to be successful in the classroom. These discussion topics should range from discipline to analysis of the teaching of one specific module or entire lesson.
4. Ask for assistance from the school system's attendance officers in visiting the homes of students who are chronically absent from school.
5. Ask teachers to post 2½-hour schedules on the wall outside the classroom doors (times that each module is taught should be on the schedule).
6. Beginning in November, notify parents that these classes are open to the public during the 2½ hours.
7. Seek the cooperation of parents in helping their children at home.
8. Check to see that books are being taken home several times a week by first graders.

The principal's third role is to build in flexibility in personnel assignments perhaps not stressed before. Such flexibility enables reassignment of support personnel at any time during the academic year to first graders who need extra help in reading and writing and in developing positive self-concepts.

The fourth role of some, but not all, principals is to examine closely their perceptions of their responsibilities. Principals who spend more time at their desks rather than with students in the classroom while supervising the ongoing instructional program must reexamine their concept of their job.

This program should have administrative support of everyone, including the superintendent. Each administrator, supervisor, and principal should read this book to gain information necessary to communicate with teachers and parents and to learn how to observe this program. *As the instructional leader of the school, the principal is also charged with making sure each teacher of this program is provided with the materials and supplies necessary to teach it.*

PARENTS

One of the best ways to work with parents is to do an effective job of teaching reading and writing. Parents must be reassured that their children will be taught to read and write. The schools must not delegate the job of teaching literacy skills to parents, since many parents cannot or will not undertake the job—they should not be expected to do so.

The school should keep parents informed through newsletters and conferences of the major areas of concentration in the instructional program. The following is an example of a newsletter to parents that might be sent home early in the academic year:

Letter to Parents

There has been local and national concern for specific educationally sound steps to be taken to improve the teaching of reading at all levels and especially at the first grade level, where a successful beginning in reading markedly affects the child's future academically. For years, many children have learned to read in the first grade; however, unfortunately, there were numbers of children who did not achieve this ability. Beginning this year, specific attention is being directed toward improving the teaching of reading and writing in ways we have not been able to accomplish in the past.

The program being taught your child encompasses the reading skills previously taught in the basal reading programs; however, in addition, we are including a very strong phonics program. Phonics will be taught each day, and during this lesson, your child will be encouraged not only to read the words but also to write them. There is a heavy emphasis on introducing children to different kinds of reading material, such as newspapers, magazines, primary-level textbooks, and library books. We do not want to limit your child only to stories found in basal readers.

To accomplish this, we seek your help and support. When possible, we would appreciate it if you would take your child to a public library, check out books, and help your child get some of the meanings from these books. In addition, we hope you will help your child in forming the letters necessary to write words. We would appreciate it if you would discuss current events in newspapers, point to key words in those stories, etc. Most of all, we want your child to enjoy this new world of reading and writing, and we hope you will not put undue pressure on your child.

As the year progresses, we believe you will see strong gains made by your child in both reading and writing; however, this will not happen by accident. It will happen as a result of the hard work of the first-grade teacher working with you and with your child.

In essence, the purpose of this program is to provide your child with the necessary skills and interests in reading. The reading and writing lessons are taught during a 2½-hour block each day, and you are invited to visit your child's classroom during this time.

The school should develop report cards that include notations about children's work in each of the major modules in this program. A brief explanation of each area should be provided to the parents. Table 8 shows a format and content for a report card that represents major aspects of the 2½ hours of daily instruction in this program.

Satisfactory improvement indicates that the student has made definite accomplishments in the specific modules since the last report card was issued.

Needs improvement indicates that the student has made some improvements in the specific modules since the last report card was issued; however, the student must concentrate on improving certain areas within the modules indicated.

Unsatisfactory improvement indicates that there is little or no difference between the work being performed currently and the work performed just prior to issuing the last report card.

The school should adopt an open-door policy and encourage parents and other interested people to visit the class, announced or unannounced, on any day during the 2½ hours of the program. Depending on which part of the program is being taught, visitors should be asked to observe quietly, assist as temporary aides while in the class, or work individually with students *according to instructions* given by the teacher. For example, visitors can assist in holding individual conferences with students, especially during the Recreational Reading Module. Parents and other visitors are encouraged to participate in this program; however, the ultimate responsibility for instruction is assumed by the professional teachers. Such visits should begin in November after the program is well underway, assuming the program was initiated in September. Approximate teaching times should be indicated on the report card, so parents can plan observation visits to the class.

The program's success should be made public. This is especially important in these days of taxpayers' revolts and emphasis on accountability. These classes should never be closed to the public.

Although parents should be encouraged to visit during class time, *this is not the time for parent-teacher conferences*. Such conferences should take place after the students leave. Since a record of each student's work is kept in the classroom in each of the five module areas, conferences with parents are expedited because parents can readily observe evidence of their child's work.

Teachers should send a *variety* of books home with the child to use in reading to parents. They should not wait until a child has mastered every word to send the book home. This program does not endorse memorization of words in the traditional sight-word approach. Instead, as soon as a student can independently decode *some* words in a book— whether in a library book, textbook, or basal reader —the book should be sent home. A note to parents should be sent with the first book explaining that the child has learned to read some, but perhaps not all, of the words in the book and requesting parents to compliment the child's success and help the child read additional parts in the book. The first books should be sent home as early as possible in the school year, according to the individual student's abilities. Teachers should not wait until an entire group of students can read a book.

TABLE 8 Suggested Reading/Writing Portions of Report Cards to Parents

INSTRUCTION MODULE EMPHASIS	MINIMUM TEACHING TIMES*	SATISFACTORY IMPROVEMENT	NEEDS IMPROVEMENT	UNSATISFACTORY IMPROVEMENT
Phonics/Spelling (associating language sounds with alphabet symbols)	9:00–9:30			
Language Experience (creating independent stories, poems, letters, and other forms of communication)	9:30–10:00			
Academic, Cultural Arts, and Current Events Reading (reading a variety of materials, such as magazines, newspapers, and textbooks, for specific purposes and using specific skills)	10:00–10:30			
Patterning (recognizing sound patterns in oral and written language)	10:30–11:00 (approximately first half of year only)			
Recreational Reading (reading of fiction and nonfiction books)	11:00–11:30 (approximately last half of year 11:00–12:00)			
Letter Formation (handwriting skills as used in all modules)				
Writing Progress (general composition as found in all modules)				

*Parents are encouraged to visit the class during the times indicated to observe the student working to improve reading and writing abilities with reference to the module emphasis.

ADDITIONAL READING

Adams, Anne H. *The Reading Clinic.* New York: Macmillan, 1970. See especially Chapter Five.

Otto, Wayne; Chester, Robert; McNeil, John; and Myers, Shirley. *Focused Reading Instruction.* Reading, Mass.: Addison-Wesley, 1974. See especially Chapter Fourteen.

chapter ten

Instructional Materials and Supplies

MATERIALS

Not only may some of the kinds of materials used in the *Success in Beginning Reading and Writing* program be different from those traditionally used in first-grade classes, but the extent of their use may differ as well. In this program, students are taught to read materials in their original form, rather than in abbreviated story excerpts, stencil copies, paragraph excerpts, and the like. Suggestions concerning uses of each of the following materials are made in the preceding chapters as well as in the lessons.

Library Books (fiction, nonfiction, poetry, reference books)

Arrangements should be made with the school librarian (as well as with a public librarian, if necessary) *to place in each first-grade classroom a minimum of thirty different fiction, nonfiction, and poetry books every three weeks*. Assuming there are thirty-six weeks in the school year, there would be twelve book placements during the year, and a minimum of 360 different library books in the classroom during the year.

In addition, students should have access to trade books that belong in the classroom and to regularly scheduled library trips to check out additional books. School policy determines whether the students can take the library books home. Hopefully, this will be permitted.

Textbooks (mathematics, science, social studies)

Since mathematics, science, and social studies textbooks are scarce in first grades, the principal and teacher will have to borrow such books either from upper-grade classrooms and/or from book storage rooms. When the books are borrowed from an upper-level classroom, that teacher should advise the first-grade teacher when the books will be needed.

These books, along with magazines and newspapers, are an essential part of the Academic, Cultural Arts, and Current Events Reading Modules. It is not necessary to have a copy of the same book for each student. In fact, it is better to have a variety of social studies, science, or mathematics textbooks.

Newspapers (class subscriptions)

The school administrators should arrange a meeting with the local newspaper publisher(s) to determine if newspapers could be purchased at a reduced rate for use in the first-grade classes. Five newspaper Monday-through-Friday subscriptions per first-grade classroom are adequate. If the local newspaper is weekly rather than daily, the number of subscriptions should be increased to ten per week per class.

Schools should also consider asking parents to donate used newspapers. Since the newspapers are marked and cut by the students, it is not feasible for several classes to share the same newspapers.

Catalogues, Various Kinds of Printed Forms, Labels, Boxes

Since catalogues are not furnished by school systems, first-grade teachers will have to request from stores, as well as from friends and parents, copies of large catalogues (Sears, J. C. Penney Co., Montgomery Ward, etc.) and smaller sales materials such as are delivered in the mail in booklet or folder format. In addition to the catalogues, collections of empty boxes, labels, forms, telephone books, and the like add other dimensions to the lessons.

Magazines (class subscriptions)

Magazine subscriptions are a definite budget item for this program, and the magazines should be used as consumable materials. Administrators should check with local magazine dealers and compare subscription costs with costs of ordering directly from the publisher.

No specific number or titles of magazines must be included; however, a recommended minimum is six different subscriptions per classroom. Those selected should include special interest, general public, and children's magazines. The following are selected magazine titles that have been used in this program:

Black Stars
Ebony, Jr.
Electric Company
Jack and Jill

National Geographic
People
Puzzle Scene
Sesame Street
Space 1999

Comic Books (class subscriptions)

Before deciding on which comic subscriptions to requisition, administrators and teachers should survey the comics available in a local store's comic rack. Generally, there are two kinds: the easier comics, such as *Casper* and *Donald Duck,* and the more difficult comics, such as *Spiderman* and *Archie.* A minimum of five comic subscriptions per class is recommended.

The following is a list of comics to consider in making subscription selections:

Believe It or Not
Bugs Bunny
Bullwinkle and Rocky
Chip and Dale
Daffy Duck
Fat Albert and the Cosby Kids
Lost in Space
Space Family Robinson
Tweety and Sylvester
Twilight Zone
Turok, Son of Stone
Underdog
Walt Disney's Comics and Stories
Walt Disney's Donald Duck
Walt Disney's Huey, Dewey, and Louie
Walt Disney's Mickey Mouse and Goofy
Walt Disney's Scamp
Yosemite Sam and Bugs Bunny

Dictionaries

Each teacher will need a paperback dictionary, and student dictionaries (not picture dictionaries) should be available. A dictionary recommended for the teacher is *The Merriam-Webster Dictionary*

(Pocket Books, latest edition). Examples of student dictionaries used in some of the classes are:

Clark, Mae Knight. *My Word-Clue Dictionary.* New York: Macmillan, 1967.

Scarry, Richard. *Richard Scarry's Fun With Words.* New York: Golden Press, 1971.

Schulz, Charles M. *The Charlie Brown Dictionary.* Englewood Cliffs, N.J.: Prentice-Hall, 1973.

Teacher-Made Materials

In the past, many teachers have spent untold hours making attractive devices for students to use in reading lessons. Although their intentions are good, teachers need not waste professional time that could be put to better advantage for the students. In this program, teachers write selected key words, phrases, and sentences supplied by the students during the Phonics/Spelling and Patterning Modules and display these charts in the classroom, preferably by the next academic day.

Teachers also have to help students record the titles of library books read or examined until students can do this independently.

The majority of other materials should be created by students. For example, in the Patterning Modules, games, wheels, flash cards, etc. should be made and used by the students in a manner that incorporates the process of creating selected instructional materials as an integral part of learning. When allowed the opportunities, students—even first graders—develop some fantastic instructional materials and are usually eager to get other students to try them out.

SUPPLIES

Paper

This program requires an ample supply of paper for each child. Some schools equipped with many of the expensive "electronic devices" for teaching do not provide students with sufficient paper to record aspects of their educational process. This program requires quite a lot of paper, and administrators should check to see that sufficient quantities for each student are provided. In selecting priorities for ordering materials with school funds, school officials should place plain, ordinary paper as a priority item.

This program includes a heavy emphasis on writing as well as reading, and there is a need for a lot of paper. Newsprint is less expensive than notebook or construction paper and is adequate for use in the textbook, magazine, and newspaper activities of the Academic, Cultural Arts, and Current Events Reading Module, the Language Experience Module, and the Recreational Reading Module. Duplicating paper will be needed for reproducing the students' Language Experience stories in the second half of the year and for other expansion activities designed by the teacher. Construction paper is needed for some of the Patterning Modules.

One idea for schools to consider exploring in securing additional unlined paper at little or no cost is to ask the Parent-Teacher Association to contact local businesses and ask them to donate paper ordinarily thrown away. Many businesses dispose of large quantities of paper printed on one side only. The other side is blank and could be used by students at any level in school. In addition, the students get a first-hand look at the kind of printed communication that goes on in local businesses. Many businesses may be glad to donate the paper to the schools.

Lined paper is to be used in the Phonics/Spelling, Patterning, and in some of the Language Experience Modules. Six reams provide 3000 sheets of lined paper. Assuming there are twenty-five students, each child can be assured of 120 sheets of lined paper during the academic year, which is considered a minimum amount.

Pencils

Each student will write with a pencil each day. The pencils should not be the larger over-sized primary pencils but should be the regular-sized pencils with erasers.

Paste, Glue, or Tape (equivalent of 9 large jars of school paste)

Paste, rather than glue or tape, seems to be the most economical and easily used material for first graders to use in lessons in this program. Although tearing and pasting can be used in all modules, the pasting is mandatory in many of the Academic, Cultural Arts, and Current Events Reading and Patterning Modules.

Scissors (optional)

Students should be encouraged to tear words, pictures, etc. from designated materials if a pair of scissors is not available for each child. This tearing/cutting/pasting may improve fine muscle coordination, provided the students, rather than the teacher, perform the tasks.

Blank Duplicating Masters

Duplicating masters are not recommended for use until the second half of the school year; however, during that time teachers will need blank masters (at least 150) on which the *students* write during the Language Experience Modules.

Manila Folders (4 per child) and 4 cardboard boxes

Each student needs a folder to file his or her written work from the Phonics/Spelling, Language Experience, Academic, Cultural Arts, and Current Events Reading, and Patterning Modules. If the budget does not permit manila folders, construction paper can be folded in half as kind of a folder. Assuming there are thirty students in the class, a minimum of 120 folders are needed.

The child's last name should be written on each folder and a class set should be alphabetized and placed in each cardboard box. One box should be labeled for each of the modules. The boxes should be placed on a table, counter, or, if necessary, the floor—not in a closet or filing cabinet. One of the first organizational responsibilities of the teacher is to prepare the four boxes of folders.

Chart Paper (1″ ruled, 27 × 34), Twine, and Clothespins

An essential component of this program is the preparation and hanging of charts in the classroom. The paper can be newsprint, poster paper, construction paper, etc., depending on the budget. Since the charts must hang individually, rather than stacked, the available space, such as bulletin boards, wall borders, and doors may be covered before all charts are hung. Some teachers have found it necessary to string twine across the classroom and use clothespins to hang the charts from the twine.

Felt Tip Pens

At least twelve felt tip pens (three of each: red, black, blue, and green) will be needed for making the charts. The size of letters made by a felt tip pen is adequate.

Phonics/Spelling Activity Sheets

Each class usually has some students who need one-to-one assistance from the teacher in *basic* reading word analysis/comprehension minilessons. Phonics/Spelling activity sheets for those students in class who cannot write or read *independently* can be purchased to accompany this program.

Before the Phonics/Spelling Module number indicated at the top of an activity sheet, the teacher should reproduce copies of the sheets for students who are having difficulty writing words volunteered by class members. During the writing phase of the module, the teacher helps these students locate the appropriate letter(s) to circle in words, in decoding, and in discussing the meanings of a few of the words. *The students should remain at their desks and not be placed in a separate group.* The teacher moves from student to student in the class and gives instruction.

The activity sheets provide an instrument that can be used by students who otherwise might be unsuccessful. As soon as students understand the letter(s)-in-words concept, basic decoding skills, and can write words independently, they should discontinue using the activity sheets. The teacher should provide other students with activity sheets if they request them.

These activity sheets are not designed to be duplicated and handed to each student and completed by students in a "busy work" manner.

Look What I Can Read and Write

Look What I Can Read and Write should be used beginning with Lesson 91 in the Recreational Reading Module on days selected by the teacher. This book is not a traditional workbook; rather, it is both a correlated language arts book and an introduction for students to the kinds of directions popular in many educational materials. For example, locating certain words, circling or underlining words, filling in blanks, etc., are standard printed directions in standardized tests and some other educational materials. Students should become comfortable with this process. Another major difference between *Look What I Can Read and Write* and other books is the absence of print on one side of each page. In addition to reading, writing, and spelling in accord with the words in the book, students add their creative selections by writing on the blank page instead of on separate sheets of paper. Here, again, the student's work is kept together for immediate and later evaluation.

COST ESTIMATES*

The following cost analysis is intended to provide administrators with some idea of initial expense of items not usually available in first-grade classes and recommended for use in this program. These figures do not include purchasing basal readers, library books, student dictionaries, or content-area textbooks that are assumed to be in the schools.

Core Program

Magazine subscription per class (*Ebony, Jr.; Jack and Jill; Sesame Street; Electric Company; People; Black Stars; Puzzle Scene; Space 1999,* etc.) $57.36

Comics subscriptions per class (*Casper, Lulu,* etc.) 28.36

Newspaper Subscriptions (5 subscriptions per class per day) 51.43

Dictionary (1 for teacher) 2.48

Success in Beginning Reading and Writing (1 for teacher) 11.95

*Approximate prices

Phonics/Spelling activity sheets (1 set per class) $3.95

Look What I Can Read and Write ($2.50 per copy. 1 copy per student) Perry-Neal Publishers, Inc., Box 2721, Durham, N.C. 27705 62.50

Supplies

Manila folders (4 per child) box of 100   5.25

Paste (9 quart jars) .76 each   6.84

10 reams duplicating paper—$1.80 each   18.00

13 reams unlined newsprint—$1.65 each (12 × 18) 21.45

8 Chart tablets—$8.65 each (50 sheets each—1″ ruled 27 × 34) 69.20

150 Duplicating Masters (1 box)   4.60

12 Felt tip pens (3 each; black, red, blue, green) 8.25

6 reams lined paper   11.10

Total cost $362.72

	Class of 25 Students	Cost per Student
Core Program	$362.72	$14.51

THE BASAL CONCEPT OF THE FUTURE

Each year, millions of taxpayers' dollars are spent on purchasing softbound and hardbound basal readers, workbooks, tests, stencils, flash cards, filmstrips, and other assorted materials related to a series. Each year, many excellent teachers bemoan the fact that they do not have a variety of materials, or even enough paper, in classrooms. In discussing the problem of how to loosen the basal grip, the question of what teachers would use if there were no basals may be raised. This program provides part of the answer to that question. Basal and supplementary readers are considered a secondary kind of reading material in this program. The students' editions are to be used as any book of short stories, and students should be encouraged to read the stories that interest them, to skip the stories that seem dull to them, and to take the books home as early and as frequently as they wish.

The teacher may select from the teacher's edition any teaching ideas that seem appropriate, interesting, and motivational for the members of each class each year and ignore the other suggestions. They should teach specific reading skills but seriously question any "scope and sequence" of reading skills. There is no evidence that one skill is more important than another or that any one reading skill must absolutely be taught before another. Teachers may give the teacher's edition to the advanced first-grade readers and let them decide which of the activities they want to complete and which of the questions they want to answer.

Basal readers have several discouraging aspects. Primary among these are some of the directions to teachers that may demean the integrity of the professionalism and intelligence. Unfortunately, teachers in basal programs are considered secondary to the program directions. Teachers are supposed to follow the instructions, even to the extent of which questions to ask the students, how to word the questions, and at which point in the lesson to ask them.

Another disadvantage of basal emphasis is the negative undercurrent of pinpointing students to work toward success in any set of books by a given grade in school at the possible expense of learning to read a variety of kinds of materials. Some excellent teachers, however, are handicapped by the prevailing notion that something will be lost if the basal lessons are not presented, and some have been confronted by principals who insist the basals be used in the classrooms.

Although great investments have been made in the traditional basal reader concept, there is no evi-

dence that continuing the dependence on the basal concept will produce other than what has been achieved in the past—a mixture of successes and failures in learning to read.

Teaching reading and learning to read can be far more exciting and interesting than any basal series or other kind of canned material. Instead of being concerned about whether a child can read the second-grade basal by the time he or she enters that grade, we should be concerned about whether the child can read a variety of books, magazine stories, mathematics lessons, newspapers, and the like.

The concept of the future, as presented in this book, is that any printed information within reason—a newspaper, a coupon, or a mathematics textbook—is a basal reading tool. *Success in Beginning Reading and Writing* encourages rather than inhibits the initiative of the professional teacher. The basic guidelines are suggested for each lesson; however, only the teacher who knows the students can determine the selection of activities and vocabulary appropriate for those students.

Until such time as we have provided first-grade classes with at least an adequate number of magazine subscriptions, newspapers, content area textbooks, classroom libraries, paper, and the like, we should not give priority to tax monies for basal and supplementary readers. We may achieve greater results without dependence on the basals.

Success in Beginning Reading and Writing Lessons

phase 1   lessons 1-10

LESSON 1

Introductory Phonics/Spelling—b

Write on chart paper words suggested by the students that contain b. Pronounce each word. Students write the letter b and words containing b. Discuss the meanings.

Examples: bat, job, banana, bumble bee, umbrella, box, basket, broom, boat.

Date and file each student's paper. Display the chart in the classroom.

Language Experience—Self: Things I Like

Write on the chalkboard words suggested by students concerning things they like. Students begin writing sentences that begin "I like . . ."

Examples of vocabulary: *big birds, go-carts, bicycles, hamburger, puppies, my mama, spaghetti, friends.*

Date and file each student's paper.

Academic, Cultural Arts, and Current Events Reading—Newspapers: b and c

Each student cuts or tears different shapes of the letters b and c from newspapers. They paste or tape the letters on their paper.

Check each student for b and c recognition.

Date and file the papers.

Patterning—bă

Write on chart paper different endings for words beginning with bă-.

Examples: <u>ba</u>d, <u>ba</u>t, <u>ba</u>ng, <u>ba</u>thtub.

Stress Emphasis: Vocal stress on one word near beginning of sentences. Display the chart in the classroom.

Student-Made Material: Each student draws a baseball bat and selects some of the words to write in the bat. Students use this material with other students.

Recreational Reading—Library Books

Help individual students find and pronounce words in library books that contain <u>b</u>.

LESSON 2

Introductory Phonics/Spelling—c.

Write on chart paper words suggested by the students that contain <u>c</u>. Pronounce each word. Students write the letter <u>c</u> and words containing <u>c</u>. Discuss the meanings.

Examples: <u>ca</u>ctus, <u>ch</u>ocolate, <u>ca</u>ke, <u>cl</u>othes, pop<u>c</u>orn, i<u>c</u>e <u>c</u>ream, <u>c</u>omb.

Date and file each student's paper. Display the chart in the classroom.

Language Experience—Self: Things I Like

Write on the chalkboard words suggested by students concerning things they like to do most. Students continue writing sentences that begin "I like . . ."

Examples of vocabulary: *chew bubble gum, jump rope, play ball, look at TV, go to McDonald's.*

Date and file each student's paper.

Academic, Cultural Arts, and Current Events Reading—Newspapers: b and c

Each student circles words in newspapers that contain <u>b</u> and/or <u>c</u>. Check each student for <u>b</u> and <u>c</u> recognition.

Date and file the papers.

Patterning—bĕ

Write on chart paper different endings for words beginning with bĕ-.

Examples: bell, better, best, best, bed, belt.

Stress Emphasis: Vocal stress on one word near medial part of sentences.

Display the chart in the classroom.

Student-Made Material: Each student draws petals on a flower and writes one of the words on some of the petals. Students use this material with other students.

Recreational Reading—Library Books

Help individual students find and pronounce words in library books that contain b.

LESSON 3

Introductory Phonics/Spelling—d

Write on chart paper words suggested by the students that contain d. Pronounce each word. Students write the letter d and words containing d. Discuss the meanings.

Examples: dog, doll, dinosaur, dynamic duo, daddy, dachshund, double decker, dollar, mad.

Date and file each student's paper. Display the chart in the classroom.

Language Experience—Self: Things I Like

Write on the chalkboard words suggested by students concerning things they like. Students draw pictures of themselves doing things and write on the pictures words for some of their actions.

Examples of vocabulary: *play football, draw, see clowns, go on trips, ride my bike*.

Date and file each student's paper.

Academic, Cultural Arts, and Current Events Reading—Magazines: Food

Students cut or tear pictures and words about different foods from magazines. They paste the pictures and words on their papers. Discuss why food is important.

Check each student for association of pictures and words with specific foods.

Date and file the papers.

Patterning—bĭ

Write on chart paper different endings for words beginning with bĭ-.

Examples: big, bib, bitter, billion.

Stress Emphasis: Vocal stress on one word near end of sentences.

Display the chart in the classroom.

Student-Made Material: Using alphabet cereal, students form bĭ words and glue the letters on paper. Students use this material with other students.

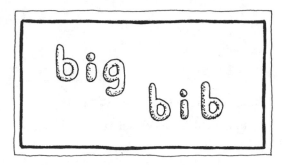

Recreational Reading—Library Books

Help individual students find and pronounce words in library books that contain b.

LESSON 4

Review Phonics/Spelling—b, c

Write on chart paper words suggested by the students that contain b, c. Pronounce each word. Students write the letters b, c and words containing b and c. Listen to each student read at least part of the chart. Discuss the meanings.

Examples: bay, belt, club, able, blood, bite, car, cartoon, cold, clean, black, crow.

Date and file each student's paper. Display the chart in the classroom.

Language Experience—Self: Things I Do

Write on the chalkboard sentences suggested by students concerning things they do. Read a sentence. Students determine which sentence was read and copy it. Repeat for three or four sentences.

Examples of vocabulary: *I can swim. I can play. I can ride my wagon.*

Date and file each student's paper.

Academic, Cultural Arts, and Current Events Reading—Magazines: Food

Students cut or tear pictures and words about food from magazines. Class discusses pictures found. Write names of food on the chalkboard. Students label their pictures from the words on the chalkboard.

Check each student for association of pictures/words with concept of food.

Date and file the papers.

Patterning—bŏ

Write on chart paper different endings for words beginning with bŏ-.

Examples: bob, body, bog, bottom, bottle, bonfire, bongo drum.

Pitch Emphasis: Raising voice near beginning of sentences.

Display the chart in the classroom.

Student-Made Material: Students draw a tree and find pictures or words containing bŏ sound. They tape or paste the pictures or words to the branches of the tree. Students use this material with other students.

Recreational Reading—Library Books

Help individual students find and pronounce words in library books that contain l.

LESSON 5

Introductory Phonics/Spelling—f

Write on chart paper words suggested by the students that contain f. Pronounce each word. Students write the letter f and words containing f. Say two words that begin with f and one word that does not have f in it. Discuss the meanings.

Examples: *frog, flip, pencil*. Ask which word does not have f in it. Do the same for words that end in -f. Make two lists of words: (1) those beginning with f-, (2) those ending with -f.

Examples: fall, five, four, flea; elf, half, self, if, off.

Compare the two lists. Say two or three words with f in the medial position.

Examples: left, after, often.

Date and file each student's paper. Display the chart in the classroom.

Language Experience—Self: Things I Do

Write on the chalkboard words suggested by students concerning things they can do. Students begin writing a story using some of these words. Sentences begin "I can . . . "

Examples of vocabulary: *sleep, paint, talk, play games, call my friend, go to the cafeteria.*

Date and file each student's paper.

Academic, Cultural Arts, and Current Events Reading—Science Textbook: Main Idea

Students in small groups explore science textbooks, locating the main idea of at least one page.

Examples of vocabulary: *the sky, the earth, planets, stars, the sun, the moon.*

Write words on the chalkboard, have students read words orally. Check each student for the main idea in one part of the textbook.

Date and file the papers.

Patterning—bŭ

Write on chart paper different endings for words beginning with bŭ-.

Examples: bud, bun, bubble, bug, bus.

Pitch Emphasis: Raising voice in medial part of sentences.

Display the chart in the classroom.

Student-Made Material: Attach a string across the chalkboard. Each student writes a word containing bu on a small piece of paper and attaches the paper to the clothesline with a clothespin. Students use this material with other students.

Recreational Reading—Library Books

Help individual students find and pronounce words in library books that contain l.

LESSON 6

Review Phonics/Spelling—d

Write on chart paper words suggested by the students that contain d. Pronounce each word. Students write the letter d and words containing d. Listen to each student read at least part of the chart. Discuss the meanings.

Examples: desk, child, card, dragon, doctor, discover, doughnut.

As a review variation, use a picture or drawing of a dog, numerous slips of paper in shape of a bone (8–10 inches), box, or bag. Write words from b chart on the "bones," and place them in box or bag (representing dog's hole). Students "dig up a bone" and read words. Write additional words suggested by students on blank bones. Students bury bones they can read. Students should copy some of the words.

Date and file each student's paper. Display the chart in the classroom.

Language Experience—Self: Things I Do

Write on the chalkboard words suggested by students. Students draw pictures of themselves doing a favorite thing. Assist labeling the objects in the pictures.

Examples of vocabulary: *make a cake, help my mother, paste things, dance, laugh.*

Date and file each student's paper.

Academic, Cultural Arts, and Current Events Reading—Science Textbook: Main Idea

Read a sentence (then a paragraph) to the class. Students tell the main ideas.

Check each student for recognition of at least one idea associated with the science content.

Date and file the papers.

Patterning—că

Write on chart paper different endings for words beginning with că-.

Examples: can, cap, cabin, cattle.

Example discussion question: *Which word beginning with că is another word for hat?*

Student-Made Material: Each student uses modeling clay and makes an object the name of which begins with că-. They write the word associated with the object.

75

Pitch Emphasis: Raising voice near end of sentences.

Display the chart in the classroom.

Possibilities of clay objects include: <u>c</u>abbage, <u>c</u>ab, <u>c</u>abinet, <u>c</u>alendar, <u>c</u>alf, <u>c</u>antaloupe, <u>c</u>amel, <u>c</u>amera, <u>c</u>andle, <u>c</u>annon, <u>c</u>anteen. Students use this material with other students.

candle   cantaloupe

Recreational Reading—Library Books

Help individual students find and pronounce words in library books that contain <u>l</u>.

LESSON 7

Introductory Phonics/Spelling—<u>g</u>

Write on chart paper words suggested by the students that contain <u>g</u>. Pronounce each word. Students write the letter <u>g</u> and words containing <u>g</u>. Discuss the meaning of the words.

Examples: <u>g</u>et, ba<u>g</u>, <u>g</u>o<u>gg</u>le, <u>g</u>reen, be<u>g</u>, <u>g</u>o-cart, <u>g</u>oldfish, <u>g</u>i<u>gg</u>le, sin<u>g</u>in<u>g</u>, <u>g</u>rill, <u>g</u>irl, <u>g</u>orilla, kan<u>g</u>aroo, oran<u>g</u>e.

Date and file each student's paper. Display the chart in the classroom.

Language Experience—Self: Things I See

Write on the chalkboard words suggested by students that they see in the classroom. Students write sentences beginning with "I see . . ."

Examples of vocabulary: *charts, pencils, paper, teacher, children, scissors, tables, rug.*

Date and file each student's paper.

Academic, Cultural Arts, and Current Events Reading—Newspapers: <u>d</u>

Students tear or cut the letter <u>d</u> and words containing <u>d</u> from newspapers and paste them on paper.

Check each student for recognition of <u>d</u>.

Date and file the papers.

Patterning—cŏ

Write on chart paper different endings for words beginning with <u>cŏ</u>-.

Examples: <u>cot</u>, <u>cotton</u>, <u>co</u>llie, <u>co</u>bweb.

Pitch Emphasis: Lowering voice near beginning of sentences.

Display the chart in the classroom.

Student-Made Material: Each group of three students uses construction paper to make a word game. They cut two holes in the paper and make strips to slide through the holes. The strip on the left is for <u>cŏ</u>; the right is for different letters that complete words beginning with <u>cŏ</u>. Students use this material with other students.

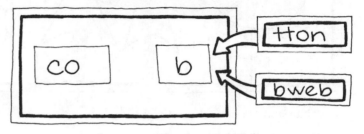

Recreational Reading—Library Books

Help individual students find and pronounce words in library books that contain <u>d</u>.

LESSON 8

Review Phonics/Spelling—<u>f</u>, <u>b</u>

Write on chart paper words suggested by the students that contain <u>f</u>, <u>b</u>. Pronounce each word. Students write the letters <u>f</u>, <u>b</u> and words containing <u>f</u>, <u>b</u>. Listen to each student read at least part of the chart. Discuss the meanings. As a review variation, students make flash cards of action words containing <u>f</u> and <u>b</u>. Students read words and make appropriate actions.

Examples: <u>f</u>ishing, <u>f</u>rying, <u>f</u>lying, playing <u>f</u>oot<u>b</u>all, <u>f</u>ollowing, sni<u>ff</u>ing; <u>b</u>atting, <u>b</u>o<u>bb</u>ing, <u>b</u>iting, <u>b</u>rushing teeth, <u>b</u>lowing <u>b</u>u<u>bb</u>les, <u>b</u>arking.

Date and file each student's paper. Display the chart in the classroom.

Language Experience—Self: Things I See

Write on the chalkboard words suggested by students of things they saw on the way to school. Students list things seen on the way to school. Write sentences with "I saw . . ." Discuss past tense.

Example of sentences: *I saw trees. I saw cars. I saw a sign.*

As a variation each student divides a sheet of paper into fourths, draws one item in each part, and writes a sentence.

Date and file each student's paper.

Academic, Cultural Arts, and Current Events Reading—Newspapers: f

Students tear or cut the letter f, words containing f, and pictures of objects the names of which contain f. Assist in labeling pictures.

Check each student for recognition of f.

Date and file the papers.

Patterning—cŭ

Write on chart paper different endings for words beginning with cŭ-.

Examples: cut, cup, cub, cuff links.

Pitch Emphasis: Lowering voice in medial part of sentences.

Display the chart in the classroom.

Student-Made Material: Each student makes at least four picture–word cards. They flash the cards to another student and make different sentences using the object on the card.

Recreational Reading—Library Books

Help individual students find and pronounce words in library books that contain d.

LESSON 9

Introductory Phonics/Spelling—h

Write on chart paper words suggested by the students that contain h. Pronounce each word. Students write the letter h and words containing h. Discuss the meanings. Decorate a box to look like a house. Place cards with words containing h in the house. Play "What do I have in the house?" by describing clues for the words. Write the words on the board. Students suggest additional words to be put in the house.

Examples: hand, horse, hammer, fish, hot dog, chicken, hello, hair, hospital, light, birthday, helicopter.

Date and file each student's paper. Display the chart in the classroom.

Language Experience—Self: Things I See

Write on the chalkboard words suggested by students concerning one object seen out the window. Students write a story about that object (trees, birds, clouds, dogs). Emphasize careful observation and description.

Date and file each student's paper.

Academic, Cultural Arts, and Current Events Reading—Magazines: Hands

Each student cuts out pictures of hands and pastes them on paper. Some tell what the hands are doing. Some may write sentences about their pictures. Check each student for association of words with concept of hands.

Date and file the papers.

Patterning—dă

Write on chart paper different endings for words beginning with dă-.

Examples: dad, dance, daffy, dagger.

Pitch Emphasis: Lowering voice near end of sentences.

Display the chart in the classroom.

Student-Made Material: Pronounce list of words, some beginning with dă- and some not. Students stand each time they hear a word beginning with dă. Additional examples: dash, dalmation, damp, dandruff, dandy. Students make flash cards and use this material with other students.

```
dash
I will dash
to the store.
```

Recreational Reading—Library Books

Help individual students find and pronounce words in library books that contain d.

LESSON 10

Review Phonics/Spelling—g, c

Write on chart paper words suggested by the students that contain g, c. Pronounce each word. Students write the letters, g, c and words containing g, c. Discuss the meanings. Review words on g chart.

Examples: good, gum, garden, garage, game, orange.

Repeat with c.

Examples: cake, carrot, black, come, juice, card.

Students write words from each list that they can read.

Date and file each student's paper. Display the chart in the classroom.

Language Experience—Self: Things I Hear

Students close eyes and listen. "What did you hear?" Write responses on the board. Children write sentences beginning "I hear . . ."

Sample sentences: *I hear people talking. I hear bells ringing. I hear dogs barking. I hear someone in the hall talking.*

Date and file each student's paper.

Academic, Cultural Arts, and Current Events Reading—Magazines: Hands

Students do hand exercises (raise hands, wiggle fingers, etc.). They cut or tear pictures of hands doing things and label the actions.

Check each student for association of words with action of hands in pictures.

Date and file the papers.

Patterning—dĕ

Write on chart paper different endings for words beginning with dĕ-.

Examples: desk, den, dent.

Juncture Emphasis: Pause near beginning of sentences.

Display the chart in the classroom.

Student-Made Material: Each student makes a deck of cards each having a word beginning with dĕ on it. Game: Child draws a card, reads it, and gives a rhyming word. Additional examples: deaf, debt, decorate, delta, deputy, desert. Students use this material with other students.

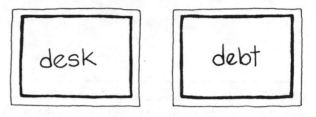

Recreational Reading—Library Books

Help individual students find and pronounce words in library books that contain m.

Success in Beginning Reading and Writing Lessons

phase 2   lessons 11-62

Beginning with Phase 2, all examples written on the Phonics/Spelling charts and on the chalkboard in the Language Experience Modules should be written in *clusters* rather than as single words. Examples on patterning charts can be single words.

LESSON 11

Introductory Phonics/Spelling—j

Write on chart paper words suggested by the students that contain j. Pronounce each word. Students write the letter j and word clusters containing j. Discuss the meanings. On the front of a large jar write the words *jelly jar*. Pull out slips of paper with the word clusters containing j. Students add other clusters and write those on the chart paper.

Examples: jumping jellybeans, jaguar from the jungle, an army jeep, junk that jingles, a joke to enjoy, jack-o-lantern.

Date and file each student's paper. Display the chart in the classroom.

Language Experience—Self: Things I Hear

Discuss the sounds things make and divide into loud sounds and soft sounds when recording suggestions on the board. Students continue writing sentences or a story.

Examples: (loud) *fire truck sirens, lion roaring, rooster crowing;* (soft) *people whispering, cats meowing, bird singing.*
Date and file each student's paper.

Academic, Cultural Arts, and Current Events Reading—Social Studies Textbook: Sequence of Events

Read a short section from the textbook. Ask students what happened in the story. Write each event on a strip of paper and put the sentences in order. Students copy the sentences in the proper order.
Check each student for what happened first, second, third, etc.
Date and file the papers.

Patterning—dĭ

Write on chart paper different endings for words beginning with dĭ-.
Examples: d̲ip, d̲izzy, d̲inner, d̲id, d̲ig, d̲isease.
Juncture Emphasis: Pause near medial part of sentences.
Display the chart in the classroom.

Student-Made Material: Small groups of students make a rhyming-word apple tree. They make at least two apples out of construction paper and write rhyming words beginning with d̲ĭ on the apples. They paste the apples on the tree.

Recreational Reading—Library Books

Help individual students find and pronounce words in library books that contain m̲.

LESSON 12

Review Phonics/Spelling—h̲, d̲

Write on chart paper words suggested by the students that contain h̲, d̲. Pronounce each word. Students write the letters h̲, d̲ and word clusters containing h̲, d̲. Use the charts from Review Lesson 6 (d̲) and Introductory Lesson 9 (h̲). Students give additional words to make clusters.

Examples: beh̲ind t̲he d̲esk, d̲angerous d̲ragon, frie̲d ch̲icken, birth̲d̲ay party, h̲ad̲ fun fish̲ing, h̲orse in t̲he h̲ouse.

Date and file each student's paper. Display the chart in the classroom.

Language Experience—Self: Things I Hear

Write on the chalkboard word clusters suggested by students concerning sounds heard on a record or tape. Students finish story or write other sentences about some of the sounds they heard.

Date and file each student's paper.

Academic, Cultural Arts, and Current Events Reading—Social Studies Textbook: Sequence of Events

Read a short story to the class and discuss the order of events. Give students paper divided into four sections. Number the sections one through four. Children draw pictures of four events in proper order and label the pictures.

Check each student for understanding of sequence.

Date and file the papers.

Patterning—d̆o

Write on chart paper different endings for words beginning with d̆o-.

Examples: d̲ollar, d̲ot, d̲octor, d̲ock.

Juncture Emphasis: Pause near end of sentences.

Display the chart in the classroom.

Student-Made Material: Small groups of students create a dot-to-dot game. Have large dot with d̆o in middle with several pieces of yarn or string attached. Around center dot place several dots with final letters on them. Connect string to each to form a word. Paper brads are good for this. Students give additional words.

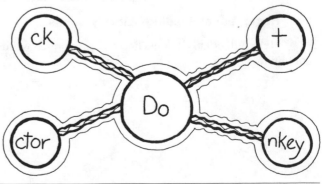

Recreational Reading—Library Books

Help individual students find and pronounce words in library books that contain m.

LESSON 13

Introductory Phonics/Spelling—k

Write on chart paper word clusters suggested by the students that contain k. Pronounce each word. Students write the letter k and word clusters containing k. Discuss the meanings. As a variation discuss *K's in the Kitchen.* List things found or done in the kitchen.

Examples: bake some cookies, drink milk, cook book, key on a hook, broken clock, dishes in the sink, mustard and ketchup.

Date and file each student's paper. Diplay the chart in the classroom.

Language Experience—Self: Things I Feel

Write on chalkboard word clusters suggested by students. Discuss feelings. Distinguish between happy feelings and unhappy feelings. Students draw faces showing different expressions. Students label the emotions represented.

Begin writing a story about feelings.

Date and file each student's paper.

happy   angry   excited

relieved   lonely   shocked

Academic, Cultural Arts, and Current Events Reading—Newspapers: G, g

Cut or tear the letters G and g and words containing these letters from the newspapers. Paste the words on paper.

Check each student for identification of G, g.

Date and file the papers.

Patterning—dŭ

Write on chart paper different endings for for words beginning with dŭ-.

Examples: duck, dull, dump.

Stress Emphasis: Vocal stress on one word near beginning of sentences.

Display the chart in the classroom.

Student-Made Material: Each student draws a picture of a rabbit on a sheet of paper. Each student makes paper carrots each containing a word beginning with dŭ-. Students use this material with other students.

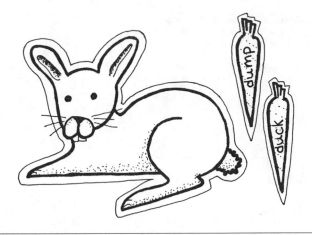

Recreational Reading—Library Books

Help individual students find and pronounce words in library books that contain s.

LESSON 14

Review Phonics/Spelling—j, f

Write on chart paper word clusters suggested by the students that contain j, f. Pronounce each word. Students write the letters j, f and word clusters containing j, f. Discuss the meanings. Review words on f chart (Lesson 5) and have students expand to clusters. Also, use action words from Lesson 8. Review clusters in jelly jar from Lesson 11. Add more suggested by students.

Examples: five fingers, flea on the frog, half of four, frying fish, jumping rope, jack-in-the-box, just a minute, juggle the balls.

Date and file each student's paper. Display the chart in the classroom.

Language Experience—Self: Things I Feel

Write on the chalkboard word clusters suggested by students concerning descriptions of items touched. Bring objects of different textures. Class decides on descriptive words for each. Attach objects to poster board and label with students' words.

Examples: *cotton = soft, sandpaper = rough, rock = hard, feather = light.*

Students continue writing a story about how things feel.

Date and file each student's paper.

**Academic, Cultural Arts, and Current
Events Reading—Newspapers: H, h**

Cut or tear the letters H and h and words containing these letters from
the newspaper. Paste the words on paper.

Check each student for identification of H, h.

Date and file the papers.

Patterning—fă

Write on chart paper different endings for
words beginning with fă.

Examples: fancy fashion, fantastic, fast falcon,
family, fact.

Stress Emphasis: Vocal stress on one word in
medial part of sentences.

Display the chart in the classroom.

Student-Made Material: Each student cuts out
of construction paper the outline of a fat person and
writes words beginning with fă on the object. Students
use this material with other students.

Recreational Reading—Library Books

Help individual students find and pronounce words in library books that
contain s.

LESSON 15

Introductory Phonics/Spelling—l

Write on chart paper word clusters suggested by the students that contain l. Pronounce each word. Students write the letter l and word clusters containing l. Discuss the meanings.

Examples: l̲ick the l̲ollipop, a l̲ighted cand̲l̲e, the l̲itt̲l̲e l̲amb, the col̲d lake, b̲lack and b̲lue, sil̲ly seal̲.

Date and file each student's paper. Display the chart in the classroom.

Language Experience—Self: Things I Feel

Write on the chalkboard word clusters suggested by students. They finish developing the story by converting some of the clusters into sentences about feelings.

Examples of vocabulary: *Ice is cold. Kittens are fuzzy. Pins are sharp. Some candy is sticky.*

Date and file each student's paper.

Academic, Cultural Arts, and Current Events Reading—Magazines: Eyes

Cut or tear pictures of eyes from a magazine. Make a group collage. Each student pastes one picture on the collage and says something about the picture.

Check each student for association of pictures with concept of eyes.

Date and file the papers.

Patterning—fĕ

Write on chart paper different endings for words beginning with fĕ-.

Examples: f̲ed, f̲eather, f̲ederal, f̲ell, f̲elt.

Stress Emphasis: Vocal stress on one word near end of sentences.

Display the chart in the classroom.

Student-Made Material: Each student writes on construction paper a sentence containing at least one word beginning with fĕ as the "Sentence of the Day" and wears the sentence that day. Students use this material with other students.

Recreational Reading—Library Books

Help individual students find and pronounce words in library books that contain s̲.

LESSON 16

Review Phonics/Spelling—k, g

Write on chart paper word clusters suggested by the students that contain k, g. Pronounce each word. Students write the letters k, g and word clusters containing k, g. Discuss the meanings. Review words on k chart. Say three words, two of which begin with k. Students tell which one doesn't. Say three words, two of which end with k. Students tell which one doesn't. Repeat the words containing k in the middle. Repeat the above with words containing g.

Examples: king, keep, back, drink, broken, spooky, goodness, gracious, swimming, rig, orange, bridge.

Date and file each student's paper. Display the chart in the classroom.

Language Experience—Environment: Animals

Write on the chalkboard word clusters suggested by students concerning descriptions of different types of animals. Students write sentences or begin stories using words and phrases written on the board.

Examples: *elephant—long trunk; kangaroo—hops; lion—hair around face; dog—my pet.*

Date and file each student's paper.

Academic, Cultural Arts, and Current Events Reading—Magazine: Eyes

Cut or tear pictures of eyes from a magazine. Discuss descriptive words. Write them on the board. Students write appropriate descriptive words on their pictures.

Check each student for association of words with concept of eyes.

Date and file the papers.

Patterning—fĭ

Write on chart paper different endings for words beginning with fi-.

Examples: fix, fib, fiddle, fifty.

Pitch Emphasis: Raising voice near beginning of sentences.

Display the chart in the classroom.

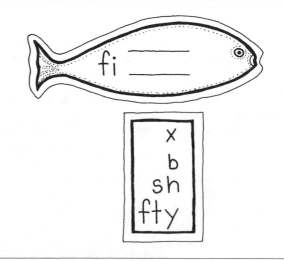

Student-Made Material: Each small group of students cuts the outline of a fish out of construction paper, cuts two slots in the paper, and cuts strips of paper that will slide through the slots. They write word endings on the strip, fi on the fish.

Recreational Reading—Library Books

Help individual students find and pronounce words in library books that contain g.

LESSON 17

Introductory Phonics/Spelling—m

Write on chart paper word clusters suggested by the students that contain m. Pronounce each word. Students write the letter m and word clusters containing m. Discuss the meanings.

Examples: mad dog, miserable cold, mistaken message, important memo.

Date and file each student's paper. Display the chart in the classroom.

Language Experience—Environment: Animals

Write on the chalkboard word clusters suggested by students concerning animals. Students draw a picture of an animal and label it using descriptive words. They continue the story or write sentences about the animal.

Date and file each student's paper.

Academic, Cultural Arts, and Current Events Reading—Mathematics Textbook: Direction Words

Students locate words in text that give directions. Teacher writes them on the board. Students read and copy.

Examples: Draw a set of _____.

Write _____.

Match _____.

Check each student for association of meaning and pronunciation of direction words.

Date and file the papers.

Patterning—fŏ

Write on chart paper different endings for words beginning with fŏ-. Write fŏ on chart paper. Make words by adding letters to the end. Find a rhyming word for each. Students suggest words and copy.

Examples: *fog–log, fox–box, follow–hollow, fond–pond.*

Pitch Emphasis: Raising voice in medial part of sentences.

Display the chart in the classroom.

Student-Made Material: Each pair of students writes and illustrates a two-line rhyming poem. Students use this material with other students.

The tree is hollow.
Go and I will follow.

The red fox
was in a big box.

Recreational Reading—Library Books

Help individual students find and pronounce words in library books that contain g.

LESSON 18

Review Phonics/Spelling—l, h

Write on chart paper word clusters suggested by the students that contain l, h. Pronounce each word. Students write the letters l, h and word clusters containing l, h. Discuss the meanings. Review l and h charts. (See Lesson 9.)

Examples: lovely hair, happy as a lark, floppy hat, horrible lunch.

Date and file each student's paper. Display the chart in the classroom.

**Language Experience—Environment:
Animals**

Write on the chalkboard word clusters suggested by students concerning pets. Teacher brings a small animal in or has a picture of an animal. Students finish the story or write sentences about the animal.

Date and file each student's paper.

**Academic, Cultural Arts, and Current
Events Reading—Mathematics Textbook:
Direction Words**

Find words that tell what to do. Write them on the board. Play "Simon Says" with the words.

Examples: *Match* the sets. *Count* the balls. *Add* the numbers.

Check each student for association of meaning and pronunciation of direction words.

Date and file the papers.

Patterning—fŭ

Write on chart paper different endings for words beginning with fŭ-.

Examples: fuzzy, fussy, funnel, fudge, fund, fungus.

Pitch Emphasis: Raising voice near end of sentence.

Display the chart in the classroom.

Student-Made Material: Each student draws a picture of a clown holding balloons. On each balloon, the student writes a word beginning with fŭ-. Students use this material with other students.

Recreational Reading—Library Books

Help individual students find and pronounce words in library books that contain g.

LESSON 19

Introductory Phonics/Spelling—n

Write on chart paper word clusters suggested by the students that contain n. Pronounce each word. Students write the letter n and word clusters containing n. Discuss the meanings. Put a large *number nine* on chart paper. On it write word clusters given by the students containing n.

Examples: finger nail, cardinal's nest, shiny needle, funny clown, seven bananas.

Date and file each student's paper. Display the chart in the classroom.

Language Experience—Environment: People

Write on the chalkboard word clusters suggested by students concerning how people are different.

Examples of vocabulary: *eye colors, first names, sounds of voices, shapes and sizes, clothes they wear.*

Students begin writing stories describing a person.

Date and file each student's paper.

Academic, Cultural Arts, and Current Events Reading—Newspapers: J, j

Students cut or tear the letters J, j and objects whose names contain these letters from the newspaper. Teacher assists in labeling the pictures.

Check each student for J, j identification.

Date and file the papers.

Patterning—gă

Write on chart paper different endings for words beginning with gă-.

Examples: gas, gag, galley, gallop, gang, gather.

Student-Made Material: Each student writes a word beginning with gă- on popsickle sticks and puts them in a paper bag. Other students "pick a stick," read the word, and make a sentence using the word. Sticks can be glued on paper to make a design.

Pitch Emphasis: Lowering voice near beginning of sentence.

Display the chart in the classroom.

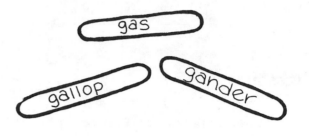

Recreational Reading—Library Books

Help individual students find and pronounce words in library books that contain r.

LESSON 20

Review Phonics/Spelling—m, j

Write on chart paper word clusters suggested by the students that contain m, j. Pronounce each word. Students write the letters m, j and word clusters containing m, j. Discuss the meanings. Students read clusters from Lessons 11, 14, and 17.

Examples: my name, a juicy melon, jumping monkey, small jockey.

Date and file each student's paper. Display the chart in the classroom.

Language Experience—Environment: People

Write on the chalkboard word clusters suggested by students describing their friends. Others guess who is being described.

Examples of vocabulary: *various interests, articles of clothing, physical features.*

Continue writing stories.

Date and file each student's paper.

Academic, Cultural Arts, and Current Events Reading—Newspapers: K, k

Students cut or tear the letters K, k and words containing these letters from newspapers.

Check each student for recognition of K, k.

Date and file the papers.

Patterning—gŏ

Write on chart paper different endings for words beginning with gŏ-.

Examples: gobble, golf, gong, goblins.

Pitch Emphasis: Lowering voice in medial part of sentence.

Display the chart in the classroom.

Student-Made Material: Students make cards with gŏ written on them. Eight students are given cards with endings written on them. One student holds a card and another student with one of the endings matches the two cards. The students pronounce the word and the process is repeated with other endings.

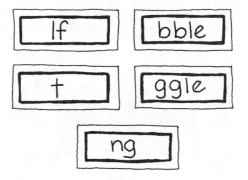

Recreational Reading—Library Books

Help individual students find and pronounce words in library books that contain r.

LESSON 21

Introductory Phonics/Spelling—p

Write on chart paper word clusters suggested by the students that contain p. Pronounce each word. Students write the letter p and word clusters containing p. Pop popcorn. Distribute popcorn when students read some of the clusters they have copied.

Examples: pat the puppy, a pretty picture, pumpkin pie, pepperoni pizza, pots and pans, popping popcorn.

Date and file each student's paper. Display the chart in the classroom.

Language Experience—Environment: People

Write on the chalkboard word clusters suggested by students concerning a member of their family. They finish writing the story and include family members in it.

Examples of vocabulary: *my mother, father works, older sister, bald uncle.*

Date and file each student's paper.

Academic, Cultural Arts, and Current Events Reading—Magazines: Feet

Students cut and paste pictures of feet on a piece of paper. Also, write words for what we do with our feet.

Examples: *run, walk, hop, stand.*

Check each student for association of words with concept of feet.

Date and file the papers.

Patterning—gŭ

Write on chart paper different endings for words beginning with gŭ-.

Examples: g<u>u</u>lf, g<u>u</u>ll, g<u>u</u>lp, g<u>u</u>mdrop, g<u>u</u>ppy, g<u>u</u>tter, g<u>u</u>st.

Pitch Emphasis: Lowering voice near end of sentences.

Display the chart in the classroom.

Student-Made Material: Use the same activity as described in Lesson 7, except use words beginning with gŭ-. Students use this material with other students.

Recreational Reading—Library Books

Help individual students find and pronounce words in library books that contain <u>r</u>.

LESSON 22

Review Phonics/Spelling—<u>n</u>, <u>k</u>

Write on chart paper word clusters suggested by the students that contain <u>n</u>, <u>k</u>. Pronounce each word. Students write the letters <u>n</u>, <u>k</u> and word clusters containing <u>n</u>, <u>k</u>. Discuss the meanings. Read clusters from Lessons 13, 16, and 19. Students incorporate some of these clusters in sentences that they read and copy.

Examples: blac<u>k</u> <u>n</u>ight, sha<u>k</u>e the pa<u>n</u>, spar<u>k</u>li<u>n</u>g <u>n</u>ec<u>k</u>lace; The <u>k</u>ing's crow<u>n</u> is o<u>n</u> the table.

Date and file each student's paper. Display the chart in the classroom.

Language Experience—Environment: Birds

Write on the chalkboard word clusters suggested by students. Show a filmstrip, play a tape, or read a story about *birds*.

Examples of vocabulary: *robin's nest, sing sweetly, watch eggs hatch, flying high.*

Students begin a story about birds.

Date and file each student's paper.

Academic, Cultural Arts, and Current Events Reading—Magazines: Feet

Cut out pictures of various animals' feet. Label feet by the animal to which they belong.

Check each student for association of words with different animals' feet.

Date and file the papers.

Patterning—hă

Write on chart paper different endings for words beginning with hă-.

Examples: half, hatchet, habit, hamster, hamburger, happen.

Juncture Emphasis: Pause near beginning of sentences.

Display the chart in the classroom.

Student-Made Material: Students make outline of hats with slots cut in each hat. Words beginning with hă- are written on strips of paper and put in the slots. Students use this material with other students.

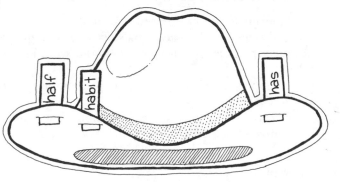

Recreational Reading—Library Books

Help individual students find and pronounce words in library books that contain y.

LESSON 23

Introductory Phonics/Spelling—q

Write on chart paper word clusters suggested by the students that contain q. Pronounce each word. Students write the letter q and word clusters containing q. Discuss the meanings. On the chart paper draw a large question mark. Discuss other clusters containing q. Point out that q is always followed by u. Students make questions from some of the clusters.

Examples: quite quiet, squeeze the squash, squat down, quit quarreling, squirrels squeak.

Date and file each student's paper. Display the chart in the classroom.

Language Experience—Environment: Birds

Write on the chalkboard word clusters suggested by students. Students draw a picture of a bird and label its parts.

Examples of vocabulary: *beak is yellow, broken wing, long tail feathers, red breast, hawk's claws.*

They continue story writing and include at least one description of a bird.

Date and file each student's paper.

Academic, Cultural Arts, and Current Events Reading—Science Textbook: Words Ending in -ing

Students locate in science books and write words on the board ending in -ing. Discuss root for each. Students copy root and word with -ing suffix. The students circle the -ing and spell each word as it is called by another student.

Examples: running, walking, jumping, hoping, talking, singing, seeing, looking, cooking, and eating.

Check each student for recognition of root words ending in -ing.

Date and file the papers.

Patterning—hĕ

Write on chart paper different endings for words beginning with hĕ-.

Examples: head, healthy, heavy, hedge, helicopter, help.

Juncture Emphasis: Pause in medial part of sentences.

Display the chart in the classroom.

Student-Made Material: Each student draws a picture of a helicopter with at least five propellers. The student writes a word beginning with hĕ- on each propeller. Students use this material with other students.

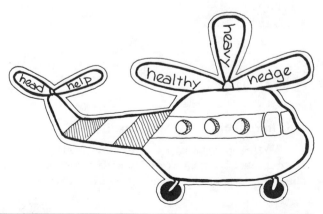

98

Recreational Reading—Library Books

Help individual students find and pronounce words in library books that contain y.

LESSON 24

Review Phonics/Spelling—p, l

Write on chart paper word clusters suggested by the students that contain p, l. Pronounce each word. Students write the letters p, l and word clusters containing p, l. Discuss the meanings. Review clusters from Lesson 15, 18, and 21.

Examples: please let me, a lot of people, purple pencil, walk in the park.

Date and file each student's paper. Display the chart in the classroom.

Language Experience—Environment: Birds

Write on the chalkboard word clusters suggested by students concerning a particular bird. Students finish the story about birds and create a bird out of the appropriate color construction paper.

Date and file each student's paper.

Academic, Cultural Arts, and Current Events Reading—Science Textbook: Words Ending in -ing

Locate words in the science textbook that end in -ing. Students write sentences with the words.

Check each student for meaning of words ending in -ing.

Date and file the papers.

Patterning—hĭ

Write on chart paper different endings for words beginning with hĭ-.

Examples: hiccup, hidden, his, hinge, hickory, history.

Juncture Emphasis: Pause near end of sentences.

Display the chart in the classroom.

Student-Made Material: Each student draws a picture of a hippopotamus on a piece of paper. Words containing hĭ are written on paper strips and pasted on the paper beside the hippopotamus. Students use this material with other students.

hidden   history   hickory

Recreational Reading—Library Books

Help individual students find and pronounce words in library books that contain y.

LESSON 25

Introductory Phonics/Spelling—r

Write on chart paper word clusters suggested by the students that contain r. Pronounce each word. Students write the letter r and words containing r. Discuss the meanings.

Examples: raise your hand, a hard rock, ran to the barn, fire truck siren, rain falls, right or wrong.

Date and file each student's paper. Display the chart in the classroom.

Language Experience—Environment: Houses

Write on the chalkboard word clusters suggested by students concerning houses. Students cut a picture of a house and label its parts.

Examples of vocabulary: *slanted roof, red brick chimney, patio door, window in front.*

Students begin a story about houses.

Date and file each student's paper.

Academic, Cultural Arts, and Current Events Reading—Newspapers: L, l

Cut or tear the letters L, l and words containing these letters from the newspaper.

Check each student for recognition of L, l.

Date and file the papers.

Patterning—hŏ

Write on chart paper different endings for words beginning with hŏ-.

Examples: hop, hockey, honk, holly, hospital.

Stress Emphasis: Vocal stress on one word near beginning of sentence.

Display the chart in the classroom.

Student-Made Material: Each student traces around circles and a triangle on a sheet of paper. Students copy words containing hŏ in designated parts of the pattern. Specified areas can then be colored. Students use this material with other students.

Recreational Reading—Library Books

Help individual students find and pronounce words in library books that contain p.

LESSON 26

Review Phonics/Spelling—q, m

Write on chart paper word clusters suggested by the students that contain q, m. Pronounce each word. Students write the letters q, m and word clusters containing q, m. Discuss the meanings. Review clusters from Lessons 17, 20 and 23. Students write sentences with some of the clusters.

Examples: mouse moves quickly, quiet morning, warm quilt, My duck quacks every day.

Date and file each student's paper. Display the chart in the classroom.

**Language Experience—Environment:
Houses**

Write on the chalkboard word clusters suggested by students about different kinds of houses. Students continue their stories and include the description of a house.

Examples of vocabulary: *building an igloo, Indian teepee, brick apartment, downtown hotel, medieval castle.*

Date and file each student's paper.

**Academic, Cultural Arts, and Current
Events Reading—Newspapers: M̲, m̲**

Cut or tear the letters M̲, m̲ and words containing these letters from the newspaper.

Check each student for recognition of M̲, m̲.

Date and file the papers.

Patterning—hŭ

Write on chart paper different endings for words beginning with hŭ-.

Examples: hug̲, hunt̲, hungry̲, hush̲, hundred̲, huddle̲.

Stress Emphasis: Vocal stress on one word in medial part of sentence.

Display the chart in the classroom.

Student-Made Material: Discuss *humps* as it relates to a camel. Each pair of students paints a camel on construction paper and makes as many *humps* containing hŭ words as possible. Students use this material with other students.

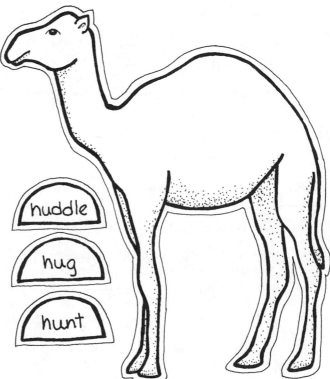

Recreational Reading—Library Books

Help individual students find and pronounce words in library books that contain p.

LESSON 27

Introductory Phonics/Spelling—s

Write on chart paper word clusters suggested by the students that contain s. Pronounce each word. Students write the letter s and words containing s. Discuss the meanings.

Examples: stars shining, steep stairs, slimy snake, sing a song, six years old, sister is sick.

Date and file each student's paper. Display the chart in the classroom.

Language Experience—Environment: Houses

Write on the chalkboard word clusters suggested by students concerning where animals live. Students finish writing their stories.

Examples of vocabulary: *bird: nest in tree, dog: wood house, fish: salt water, ant: anthills of sand.*

Date and file each student's paper.

Academic, Cultural Arts, and Current Events Reading—Magazines: Television

Students draw a picture of a television set. They cut pictures and words from magazines that they can associate with television, glue them to their pictures.

Check each student for association of words with concept of television.

Date and file the papers.

Patterning—jă

Write on chart paper different endings for words beginning with jă-.

Examples: jam, jab, jacks, jazz, jaguar, jack-o-lantern.

Stress Emphasis: Vocal stress on one word near end of sentences.

Display the chart in the classroom.

Student-Made Material: Each student draws and cuts a jack-o-lantern from construction paper. These are then taped to popsicle sticks. Students copy words containing jă on the jack-o-lantern. Working with a partner, students hold up their jack-o-lanterns and give their partner the opportunity to pronounce words.

Recreational Reading—Library Books

Help individual students find and pronounce words in library books that contain p.

LESSON 28

Review Phonics/Spelling—r, n

Write on chart paper word clusters suggested by the students that contain r, n. Pronounce each word. Students write the letters r, n and word clusters containing r, n.

Examples: read the newspaper, right now, orange sunset, brown raccoon.
Date and file each student's paper. Display the chart in the classroom.

Language Experience—Environment: Furniture

Write on the chalkboard word clusters suggested by students concerning furniture. Students suggest names of furniture that are then written on the board. Discuss purpose of each.

Examples: *kitchen table, lounge chair, chest of drawers, living room sofa.*
Students begin a story about furniture.
Date and file each student's paper.

Academic, Cultural Arts, and Current Events Reading—Magazines: Television

Students find pictures and words about television in magazines. They write sentences under these telling their favorite program.

Check each student for association of words with concept of television.

Date and file the papers.

Patterning—jĕ, jĭ

Write on chart paper different endings for words beginning with jĕ, jĭ.

Examples: jet, jester, jealous; jiffy, jinx, jigsaw, jitter.

Pitch Stress: Raising voice near beginning of sentences.

Display the chart in the classroom.

Student-Made Material: Same as Lesson 12 except use words containing jĕ and jĭ. Students use this material with other students.

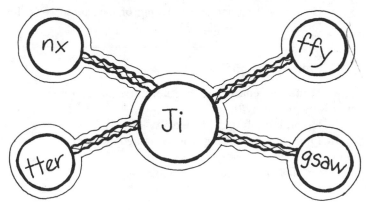

Recreational Reading—Library Books

Help individual students find and pronounce words in library books that contain f.

LESSON 29

Introductory Phonics/Spelling—t

Write on chart paper word clusters suggested by the students that contain t. Pronounce each word. Students write the letter t and word clusters containing t. Discuss the meanings.

Examples: on telephone, tick-tack-toe, a flat tire, two tiny turtles, terrible picture, three teeth out.

Date and file each student's paper. Display the chart in the classroom.

**Language Experience—Environment:
Furniture**

Write on the chalkboard word clusters suggested by students concerning furniture. Class classifies them according to room in which they belong.

Examples of vocabulary: *double bed, chest of drawers, velvet couch, dining table.*

Students continue writing stories about furniture.

Date and file each student's paper.

**Academic, Cultural Arts, and Current
Events Reading—Social Studies Textbook:
Words Ending in -ed**

Locate and write words from social studies textbooks that end in -ed. Briefly discuss present versus past tense.

Check each student for meaning of past tense verbs found.

Date and file the papers.

Patterning—jŏ

Write on chart paper different endings for words beginning with jŏ-.

Examples: job, jot, jog, jockey, jolly.

Pitch Stress: Raising voice in medial part of sentences.

Display the chart in the classroom.

Student-Made Material: Each student draws a sad clown. In order to make the clown jolly, words containing jŏ must be written on the clown. Each student reads his or her jŏ words to a friend.

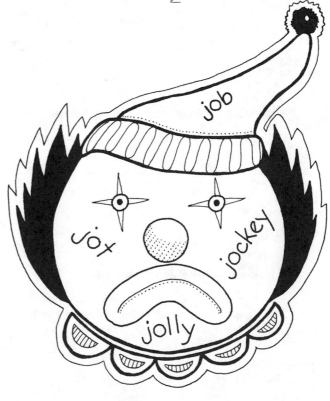

Recreational Reading—Library Books

Help individual students find and pronounce words in library books that contain f.

LESSON 30

Review Phonics/Spelling—s, p

Write on chart paper word clusters suggested by the students that contain s, p. Pronounce each word. Students write the letters s, p and word clusters containing s, p. Discuss the meanings. Review clusters from Lessons 21, 24 and 27. Students write sentences with some of the clusters.

Examples: sticky peppermint stick, soap powder, potato salad, salt and pepper are spices.

Date and file each student's paper. Display the chart in the classroom.

Language Experience—Environment: Furniture

Write on the chalkboard word clusters suggested by students concerning furniture. Students describe on paper the furniture in one room and finish their stories about furniture. Illustrate with pictures drawn or cut from magazines.

Examples of vocabulary: *leather chair, dressing table, four-drawer dresser, study lamp.*

Date and file each student's paper.

Academic, Cultural Arts, and Current Events Reading—Social Studies Textbook: Words Ending in -ed

Locate and write on board words that end in -ed. Continue discussion of past and present tense. Change verbs from one tense to the other. Write sentences. Have the students copy.

Check each student for meaning of past-tense verbs.

Date and file the papers.

Patterning—jŭ

Write on chart paper different endings for words beginning with jŭ-.

Examples: junk, just, jug, juggle, judge, jungle.

Pitch Stress: Raising voice near the end of sentences.

Display the chart in the classroom.

Student-Made Material: A small group of students (3–4) creates a picture by pasting *junk* (buttons, paper strips, straws, etc.) on construction paper. Be sure to discuss meaning of *junk.*

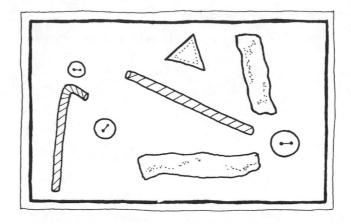

Recreational Reading—Library Books

Help individual students find and pronounce words in library books that contain <u>f</u>.

LESSON 31

Introductory Phonics/Spelling—<u>v</u>

Write on chart paper word clusters suggested by the students that contain <u>v</u>. Pronounce each word. Students write the letter <u>v</u> and word clusters containing <u>v</u>. Discuss the meanings.

Examples: <u>velvet vest, vampire bat, Laverne</u> and Shirley, I lo<u>ve</u> you.

Date and file each student's paper. Display the chart in the classroom.

**Language Experience—Environment:
Toys**

Write on the chalkboard word clusters suggested by students concerning toys. Students cut pictures of toys from magazines. Class groups them as to "indoor" or "outdoor" toys. Each child pastes a toy on a poster of *Indoor Toys* and one of *Outdoor Toys*. Each picture is labeled by name.

Examples of vocabulary: *baby doll, dump truck, basketball hoop, electric train.*

Students begin writing a story about toys.

Date and file each student's paper.

**Academic, Cultural Arts, and Current
Events Reading—Newspapers: <u>N</u>, <u>n</u>**

Cut or tear the letters <u>N</u>, <u>n</u> and words containing them from the newspaper.

Check each student for recognition of N, n.
Date and file the papers.

Patterning—kĕ

Write on chart paper different endings for words beginning with kĕ-.

Examples: keg, kept, kettle, ketchup, kennel.

Pitch Stress: Lowering voice near beginning of sentences.

Display the chart in the classroom.

Student-Made Material: Each pair of students draws a large bottle of ketchup on a piece of paper. Then they draw foods on which they like to eat ketchup. Two pairs of students get together and discuss their drawings.

Recreational Reading—Library Books

Help individual students find and pronounce words in library books that contain x or z.

LESSON 32

Review Phonics/Spelling—t, q

Write on chart paper word clusters suggested by the students that contain t, q. Pronounce each word. Students write the letters t, q and word clusters containing t, q. Discuss the meanings. Review clusters from Lessons 23, 26, and 29. Students write sentences with some clusters.

Examples: What's the question?, Tickets cost a quarter., little squirrel, quit talking.

Date and file each student's paper. Display the chart in the classroom.

**Language Experience—Environment:
Toys**

Write on the chalkboard word clusters suggested by students concerning toys. Students cut pictures of toys from magazines and continue writing stories about toys.

Examples: *The race cars will go fast. The fire engine has three ladders.*

Date and file each student's paper.

**Academic, Cultural Arts, and Current
Events Reading—Newspapers: <u>P</u>, <u>p</u>**

Cut or tear the letters <u>P</u>, <u>p</u> and words containing these letters from the newspapers.

Check each student for recognition of <u>P</u>, <u>p</u>.

Date and file the papers.

Patterning—k<u>ĭ</u>

Write on chart paper different endings for words beginning with k<u>i</u>-.

Examples: <u>ki</u>d, <u>ki</u>ck, <u>ki</u>ll, <u>ki</u>tchen, <u>ki</u>dnap, <u>ki</u>ng.

Pitch Stress: Lowering voice in medial part of sentences.

Display the chart in the classroom.

Student-Made Material: Students work in small groups (3–4) and using popped popcorn make a picture of one of the words containing k<u>ĭ</u> by glueing popcorn on construction paper.

Examples: <u>ki</u>d, <u>ki</u>ck, <u>ki</u>tchen, <u>ki</u>ng, <u>ki</u>tten.

Recreational Reading—Library Books

Help individual students find and pronounce words in library books that contain <u>x</u> or <u>y</u>.

Beginning with Lesson 33, only the module variations appear in the following lessons. The formats introduced in prior lessons continue. In the Phonics/Spelling Modules, the teacher continues to begin each module by creating a chart containing clusters of words suggested by students. They write some of the clusters during the module, the chart is displayed, and the students' papers are dated and filed. An "introductory device" is suggested to stimulate discussions. In the Language Experience Modules the three-day development of a story continues. Only additional suggestions to the basic format appear in the following modules. In the Academic, Cultural Arts, and Current Events Reading Modules, the teacher should continue to check each student's identification of information found with the theme of the module. The Patterning Modules suggest manipulative devices or art items. The teacher should decide if individual students, small groups, or the entire class should create the object. Some of the Patterning Modules suggest ways to vary the beginning of the modules.

LESSON 33

Introductory Phonics/Spelling—w

Write on chart paper word clusters suggested by the students that contain w. Pronounce each word. Students write the letter w and word clusters containing w. Discuss the meanings.

Examples: windy weather, wishing well, white woodwork, wicked witch, a wet towel, walk with me.

Date and file each student's paper. Display the chart in the classroom.

Language Experience—Environment:
Toys

Students draw a picture of their favorite toy and write a story about it.
Examples: *I feed my doll with a bottle. I ride my bicycle on the sidewalk.*

Academic, Cultural Arts, and Current
Events Reading—Magazine: Money

Introduce $ and ¢. Students cut from magazines amounts of money written with these signs. Discuss relative value of amounts found.

Patterning—la

Make words beginning with la-. Discuss meanings.
Examples: lap, last, land, lamp, ladder, lantern.

Student-Made Material: Each student forms object containing la words from wire and/or pipe cleaners. Objects are stapled on styrofoam. The name of the object is written on a strip of paper and stapled to the styrofoam. Students use this material with other students.

111

Recreational Reading—Library Books

Find and pronounce words containing x or z.

LESSON 34

Review Phonics/Spelling—v, r

Review clusters from Lessons 25, 28, and 31. Students give other clusters. Students write sentences with some clusters.
Examples: valuable ring, sick with fever, lovely purple violets.

Language Experience—Food: Breakfast

Discuss what students had for breakfast. Make a list on the board. Students should copy.
Examples of vocabulary: *hot oatmeal, a bowl of cereal, glass of milk, cinnamon toast.*

Patterning—le

Introductory device: Have children stand on their left leg.
Examples: let, letter, lesson, lend, lead, leather.

Student-Made Material: Each student will use yarn, construction paper, and glue to form *letters* that the teacher calls out.
Examples: Form a letter that has a straight line, a letter that is a circle, a letter in your name.
Students use this material with other students.

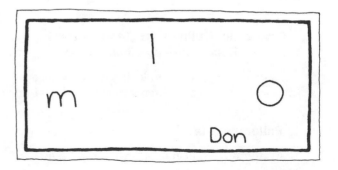

Recreational Reading—Library Books

Find and pronounce words containing o̲.

LESSON 35

Introductory Phonics/Spelling—x̲

Introductory device: Very large *exclamation mark*. Discuss relationship to *excitement*. Write clusters on exclamation mark. Discuss the meanings.

Example: six̲ box̲es, chicken pox̲, ex̲cellent work, box̲ing ex̲ercises, cake mix̲, wax̲ the car.

Language Experience—Food: Breakfast

Discuss a well-balanced *breakfast*. Students find or draw pictures of a good breakfast and label them.

Examples of vocabulary: *eggs with sausage, orange juice, buttered toast.*

Academic, Cultural Arts, and Current Events Reading—Magazines: Money

Students cut three items from magazines and paste them in order of relative cost.

Patterning—lĭ

Make words beginning with lĭ-. Discuss meanings.

Examples: l̲ick, l̲id, l̲ift, l̲imb, l̲imit, l̲iquid.

Student-Made Material: Students work in small groups (3–4) and make a collage using pictures from magazines to illustrate words containing lĭ. Collages can be joined and displayed

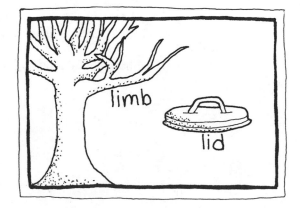

Recreational Reading—Library Books

Find and pronounce words containing o.

LESSON 36

Review Phonics/Spelling—s, w

Review clusters from Lessons 27, 30, and 33. Students give other clusters. Discuss the meanings. Students write sentences with some clusters.

Examples: rinse water, fish swim, wash your hands, soap powder.

Language Experience—Food: Breakfast

Each student writes a story about what he or she had for breakfast. Assist in spelling.

Examples: *I had waffles with syrup. I ate everything because I was hungry.*

Academic, Cultural Arts, and Current Events Reading—Mathematics Textbook: Specialized Words

Look for other key words in math book. Record, discuss, read.

Examples: *row, which one, number words, each.*

Patterning—lŏ, lŭ

1. Introductory device: a lock requiring a key; several keys, one of which opens the lock. Student who suggests a word beginning with lŏ- gets to try a key.

Examples: log, long, lost, lobby, lobster, lodge.

2. One who opens lock is *lucky*. Discuss words beginning with lŭ-.

Examples: lump, lumber, lug, lullaby, luggage, lung.

Student-Made Material: Students work in small groups (3–4) and cut out patterns of eggs. A word containing lŏ or lŭ is written on the top part of the egg and a picture representing the word is drawn on the bottom half of the egg. Each egg is then cut apart in a zigzag fashion. The groups trade eggs and put the eggs together, associating word and picture.

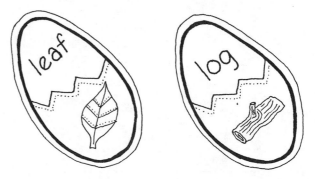

Recreational Reading—Library Books

Find and pronounce words containing o.

LESSON 37

Introductory Phonics/Spelling—y

Introductory device: yellow keys. Write clusters on yellow keys and discuss the meanings. Students give other clusters containing y.

Examples: snowy day, play in your yard, sleepy yawn, a toy yo-yo, baby crying, yesterday was cloudy.

Language Experience—Food: Lunch

Students suggest foods for lunch. Class categorizes them into breads, vegetables, meat, fruit, dessert. Students copy lists.

Examples of vocabulary: *fresh peaches, blueberry pie, sweet corn, rolls with butter.*

Academic, Cultural Arts, and Current Events Reading—Newspaper: Q, q

Cut or tear the letters Q, q and words containing them from the newspaper.

Patterning—mă

Make words beginning with mă-. Discuss meanings.

Examples: mad, magnet, matter, man, map, marry.

Student-Made Material: Each student draws a large magnet on a piece of paper and writes words containing mă. Students use this material with other students.

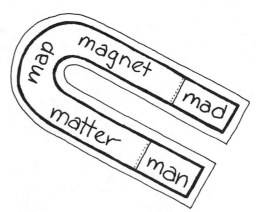

Recreational Reading—Library Books

Find and pronounce words containing q.

LESSON 38

Review Phonics/Spelling—x, t

Review clusters from Lessons 29, 32, and 35. Students give other clusters. Students write sentences with some of the clusters.
Examples: tax money, take a taxi, out the exit, chest x-ray.

Language Experience—Food: Lunch

Discuss the meaning of "menu." Plan a menu for lunch.
Examples: *cup of soup, ham sandwich, piece of fruit, green beans, chocolate milk.*

Academic Cultural Arts, and Current Events Reading—Newspaper: R, r

Cut or tear the letters R, r and words containing them from the newspaper.

Patterning—mĕ

Introductory device: pictures of rooms, clothes, etc., in a mess.
Examples: melt, met, metal, medal, memory, measure.

Student-Made Material: Each student draws and cuts out a leaf and writes one of the words containing mĕ on the leaf. Using yarn, students create mobiles with the leaves. Students use this material with other students.

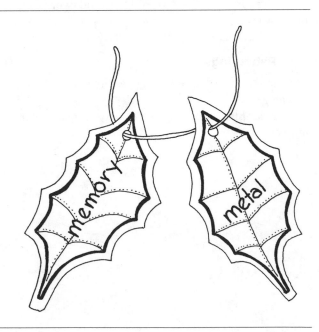

Recreational Reading—Library Books

Find and pronounce words containing q.

LESSON 39

Introductory Phonics/Spelling—z

Introductory device: On poster board draw a large lizard. Cut it into six or eight pieces forming a puzzle. Write clusters on the pieces. The class assembles the puzzle as it reads the clusters.

Examples: *zebra in the zoo, I'm dizzy, zigzag lines, size zero, the zooming car, fuzzy rabbit.*

Language Experience—Food: Lunch

Students cut out pictures of what they had or would like for lunch, paste them on a paper plate, and label them.

Examples of vocabulary: *hot buttermilk biscuits, chopped spinach, chicken salad, french fries.*

Academic, Cultural Arts, and Current Events Reading—Magazine: Water

Discuss different places water is found: *ocean, pond, waterfall, river, rain.* Find a picture of each and label.

Patterning—mĭ

Make words beginning with mĭ-. Discuss meanings.

Examples: <u>mi</u>ss, <u>mi</u>lk, <u>mi</u>ddle, <u>mi</u>tt, <u>mi</u>dnight, <u>mi</u>llion, <u>mi</u>x.

Student-Made Material: Each student will use finger paint and create a design. Give each student two different colors of paint to mix together. Designs can be displayed. Students use this material with other students.

I <u>mixed</u> green and blue.

Recreational Reading—Library Books

Find and pronounce words containing q.

LESSON 40

Review Phonics/Spelling—y, v

Review clusters from Lessons 31, 34, and 37. Students give other clusters. Students write sentences with some clusters.

Examples: very funny, lady, play a violin, eat your vegetable, saving money.

Language Experience—Food: Dinner

Discuss different foods eaten for dinner. Categorize according to breads, vegetables, fruit, meat, desserts, drinks.

Examples: *roast beef, cooked cabbage, chocolate cake, broccoli in cheese sauce.*

Academic, Cultural Arts, and Current Events Reading—Magazine: Water

Discuss different uses of water: *drinking, cooking, cleaning, swimming, watering plants, traveling on.* Find pictures to illustrate these uses.

Patterning—mŏ

Introductory device: picture of a monster.

Examples: moth, mom, mop, model, modern, mockingbird.

Student-Made Material: Each student traces around his hand, creates a monster and copies words containing mŏ. Students use this material with other students.

Recreational Reading—Library Books

Find and pronounce words containing w.

LESSON 41

Introductory Phonics/Spelling—a

Introductory device: Magician with a black hat. Class says, "Abracadabra" as a child pulls a cluster from the hat. Students suggest other clusters.

Examples: bacon for breakfast, a lamp shade, carry a bag, a bad headache, Mama baking a cake, astronaut in space.

Language Experience—Food: Dinner

Make a booklet of types of foods. Draw or cut out pictures. Label. Each page should be one category from Lesson 40.

Examples: *fried chicken, potato salad, spiced applesauce, glass of milk.*

Academic, Cultural Arts, and Current Events Reading—Science Textbook: Specialized Words

Find and write specialized words from a lesson in a science textbook.
Examples: *cold, solid, evaporate, steam, liquid.*

Patterning—mŭ

Make words that begin with mŭ-. Discuss meanings.

Examples: mud, muck, muffler, muscle, mummy, mutt.

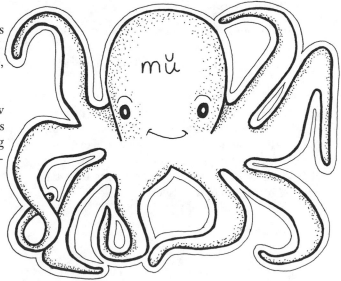

Student-Made Material: Each student will draw an octopus on a sheet of paper and write the letters mŭ on the head. Endings, forming words beginning with mŭ-, are written on the legs of the octopus. Students use this material with other students.

Recreational Reading—Library Books

Find and pronounce words which contain w.

LESSON 42

Review Phonics/Spelling—z, w

Review clusters from Lessons 33, 36, and 39. Students give other clusters. Students write sentences with some clusters.

Examples: jigsaw puzzle, write your zip code, crazy way to go, black and white zebra.

Language Experience—Food: Dinner

Students describe a favorite dinner. Help with spelling.

Examples of vocabulary: *slice of ham, acorn squash, cornbread with butter, tapioca pudding.*

Academic, Cultural Arts, and Current Events Reading—Science Textbook: Specialized Words

Locate and write words pertaining to a specific science lesson.

Example: *Weather—snow, rain, hail, thunder.*

Patterning—nă

Introduction: Discuss nap as a short sleep in daytime.

Examples: nab, nag, nanny, national, natural.

Student-Made Material: Each student thinks of something he or she would dream during a nap. These dreams are illustrated in designs made by straw painting. A small amount of tempera paint is placed on a piece of construction paper. Place the straw at an angle and blow in any direction. Students then talk about their dream to other students.

Recreational Reading—Library Books

Find and pronounce words containing w̲.

LESSON 43

Introductory Phonics/Spelling—e̲

Introductory device: a huge elephant.

Examples: fir̲e̲ e̲ngin̲e̲, a gre̲en le̲af, all e̲xcept me̲, e̲asy re̲ad̲e̲r, re̲ad th̲e̲ n̲ewspap̲e̲r, e̲xcell̲e̲nt work.

Language Experience—Food: Taste

Write on the board: *Sweet, bitter, sour, salty.* Students give foods for each category. Students copy.

Examples of vocabulary: *slice of lemon, chocolate cookie, bag of peanuts, Chinese tea.*

Academic, Cultural Arts, and Current Events Reading—Newspaper: S̲, s̲

Cut or tear the letters S̲, s̲ and words containing them from the newspaper.

Patterning—n̲ĕ

Make words that begin with n̲ĕ-. Discuss meanings.

Examples: n̲eck, n̲est, n̲ext, n̲et, n̲ephew, n̲ecessary.

Student-Made Material: Each pair of students will be given a picture of a giraffe and will write words containing n<u>ĕ</u> on the giraffe. Pictures are exchanged with another pair of students. Words containing n<u>ĕ</u> are pronounced and sentences containing these words are given.

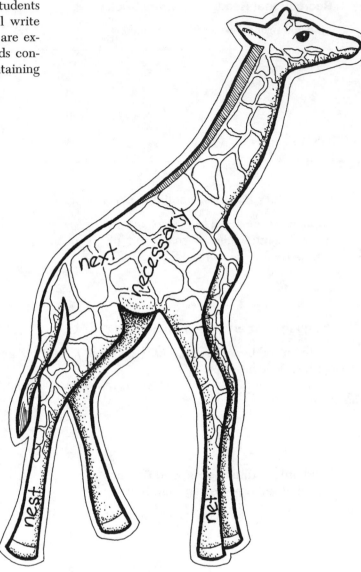

Recreational Reading—Library Books

Find and pronounce words containing <u>e</u>.

LESSON 44

Review Phonics/Spelling—a, x

Review clusters from Lessons 35, 38, and 41. Students suggest other clusters and write sentences with some.
Examples: a sharp axe, wax the floor, taxi cab, sales tax.

Language Experience—Food: Taste

Students name several foods and write sentences about how each tastes.
Examples: *Oranges are juicy and sweet. Most crackers are salty.*

Academic, Cultural Arts, and Current Events Reading—Newspaper: T, t

Cut or tear the letters T, t and words containing them from the newspaper.

Patterning—nĭ

Introductory device: nickle.
Examples: nip, nibble, nitwit, nitty-gritty, nifty.

Student-Made Material: Each student will make a *nifty* picture (discuss meaning) out of yarn. The student will sketch a picture on stiff paper and paste yarn over the picture. Students discuss pictures with other students.

Recreational Reading—Library Books

Find and pronounce words containing e.

LESSON 45

Introductory Phonics/Spelling—i

Introductory device: Picture of Eskimos who live in igloos that are made of ice.

123

Example: he <u>i</u>s <u>i</u>ll, n<u>i</u>ne <u>inni</u>ngs, van<u>i</u>lla <u>i</u>c<u>i</u>ng, <u>i</u>ron your sh<u>i</u>rt, qu<u>ie</u>t l<u>i</u>ttle k<u>i</u>tten, wh<u>i</u>te napk<u>i</u>ns.

Language Experience—Food: Taste

Good food tastes _____. Students supply words.
Examples: *yummy, sweet, hot, cold, delicious.*
Students write sentences telling a food that can be described by each word.
Examples: *Milk is cold. Candy is sweet.*

Academic, Cultural Arts, and Current
Events Reading—Magazine: Birds

Students tear or cut pictures of birds from magazines and label them with words describing the appearance or parts of the birds.

Patterning—n<u>ŏ</u>, n<u>ŭ</u>

Make words which begin with n<u>ŏ</u>- and n<u>ŭ</u>-. Discuss meanings.
Examples: <u>nod</u>, <u>not</u>, <u>noggin</u>, <u>novelty</u>; <u>nut</u>, <u>nutty</u>, <u>nun</u>, <u>number</u>.

Student-Made Material: Each student writes a word containing n<u>ŏ</u> or n<u>ŭ</u> on a card and places it in a large jar. Students take turns selecting a card from the jar and pronouncing it. If correct, they can keep the word card.

Recreational Reading—Library Books

Find and pronounce words containing <u>e</u>.

LESSON 46

Review Phonics/Spelling—e̲, y̲

Review clusters from Lessons 37, 40, and 43. Students suggest other clusters and write sentences with some.

Examples: e̲yes to s̲e̲e̲, e̲njoy̲ y̲ourse̲lf, e̲mpty̲ e̲levator, e̲nd of the̲ da̲y̲.

Language Experience—Food: Colors

Discuss foods of various colors. Students make a booklet with one color per page. They draw or cut out pictures of food for each page and label food.

Examples: *red—ripe tomatoes, hot radishes; yellow—fresh squash, sweet corn; green—string beans, crisp lettuce.*

Academic, Cultural Arts, and Current Events Reading—Magazines: Birds

Students paste on paper pictures of birds doing different things. They write sentences about what the birds are doing.

Examples: *The bird is flying. The blue bird is sitting on his nest.*

Patterning—pā

Read "Jack and Jill." Discuss *pail*. Students suggest other words beginning with p̲ā.

Examples: p̲age, p̲aper, p̲ay, p̲aint, p̲aste.

Student-Made Material: Each student will draw or write a use of a pail (to step on, to carry water in). These are discussed and placed in a pail and kept in the classroom for children to read and share.

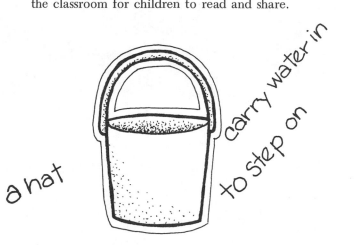

Recreational Reading—Library Books

Find and pronounce words containing n̲.

LESSON 47

Introductory Phonics/Spelling—o

Introductory device: Octopus that lives in the ocean. Write clusters on legs.

Examples: ch<u>o</u>colate c<u>o</u>okies, h<u>oo</u>t <u>o</u>wl, <u>o</u>n the r<u>oo</u>f, <u>o</u>pen the d<u>oo</u>r, goldfish b<u>ow</u>l, p<u>o</u>lice <u>o</u>fficer.

Language Experience—Food: Colors

Students write sentences about different colors of food.
Examples: *A banana is yellow. Cucumbers are green.*

Academic, Cultural Arts, and Current Events Reading—Social Studies Textbook: Items in Pictures

Students find words in print of items illustrated in pictures. Write on board. Students read and copy.

Patterning—pē

Make words that begin with p<u>ē</u>. Discuss meanings.
Examples: <u>pee</u>l, <u>pea</u>ch, <u>peo</u>ple, <u>pea</u>ce, <u>pea</u>nut.

Student-Made Material: An outline of each student will be traced on sheet of butcher paper and then student will fill in details. Discuss different characteristics of people. Display paper people in the classroom. Students write words beginning with p<u>ē</u> on them. Students use this material with other students.

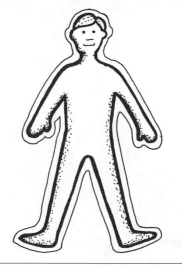

Recreational Reading—Library Books

Find and pronounce words containing <u>n</u>.

LESSON 48

Review Phonics/Spelling—i, z

Review clusters from Lessons 39, 42, and 45. Students suggest other clusters and write sentences with some.

Examples: dri<u>zzl</u>ing ra<u>in</u>, s<u>ill</u>y ch<u>i</u>mpan<u>zee</u>, p<u>izz</u>a p<u>ie</u>, maga<u>zi</u>ne p<u>i</u>cture.

Language Experience—Food: Colors

Discuss colors of fruit. Make a list of fruit. Children categorize by color on their paper.

Examples: *red—delicious apple, yellow—ripe banana, purple—plum from the tree, green—slice of lime.*

Academic, Cultural Arts, and Current Events Reading—Social Studies Textbook: Items in Pictures

Read and discuss relationship of captions and the pictures they describe. Discuss main idea presented.

Patterning—pī

On a large pie divided into sections, write words that begin with pī-.

Examples: <u>pi</u>le, <u>pi</u>pe, <u>pi</u>lot, <u>pi</u>nt, <u>pi</u>ne.

Student-Made Material: Each student draws a pie and divides it into sections. A word containing pī- is written on each section. Sections are cut apart and students match their sections with other students' identical sections. Word pairs can be displayed.

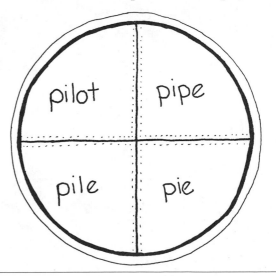

Recreational Reading—Library Books

Find and pronounce words containing <u>n</u>.

LESSON 49

Introductory Phonics/Spelling—u

Introductory device: a blue umbrella.
Examples: ugly duckling, understand the rules, Bugs Bunny, the slow turtle, nurse's uniform, under the ground.

Language Experience—Animals: Dogs

Discuss and write sentences about things dogs can do. Examples: *bark loudly, fetch things, run fast, bite people.*

Academic, Cultural Arts, and Current Events Reading—Newspapers: V, v

Cut or tear the letters V, v and words containing them from the newspaper.

Patterning—pō

Make words that begin with pō-. Discuss meanings.
Examples: poem, Poland, polar bear, pony, post.

Student-Made Material: Each group of three or four students creates and illustrates a simple poem containing as many pō words as possible. These are shared with other students.
Example:
Our poem will be about a
  polar bear
And a hare
Who sat on a post
To watch a ghost.

Recreational Reading—Library Books

Find and pronounce words containing v.

LESSON 50

Review Phonics/Spelling—<u>o</u>, <u>a</u>

Review clusters from Lessons 41, 44, and 47. Students suggest other clusters and write sentences with some.

Examples: <u>a</u>nother aftern<u>oo</u>n, <u>a</u> m<u>a</u>gic b<u>o</u>x, yell<u>o</u>w cr<u>ay</u>on, <u>a</u>irpl<u>a</u>ne pil<u>o</u>t.

Language Experience—Animals: Dogs

Discuss and write about different physical features of dogs.
Examples: *shaggy hair, floppy ears, short legs, sad eyes.*

Academic, Cultural Arts, and Current Events Reading—Newspaper: <u>W</u>, <u>w</u>

Cut or tear the letters <u>W</u>, <u>w</u> and words containing them from the newspaper.

Patterning—r<u>ā</u>

Introductory device: a rainbow.
Examples: <u>ra</u>ce, <u>ra</u>dio, <u>ra</u>ilroad, <u>ra</u>ise, <u>ra</u>y, <u>ra</u>diator.

Student-Made Material: Each student will create a rainbow using fingerpaint. Students use this material with other students.

Recreational Reading—Library Books

Find and pronounce words containing <u>v</u>.

LESSON 51

Introductory Phonics/Spelling—<u>A</u>, <u>B</u>

Discuss need to capitalize all names. Students give name clusters beginning with <u>A</u> and <u>B</u> and tell which of each is the name.

Examples: Alice in Wonderland, African jungle, arid Arizona, Atlantic Ocean, April showers, Ajax Cleanser, Buffalo Bob, Buffalo Braves, Big Ben, Bacon Street, the city of Baltimore, Bill's book.

Language Experience—Animals: Dogs

Students write a story about a dog they have or would like to have. Help with spelling.

Examples of vocabulary: *wags his tail, spotted face, dog house, hides a bone.*

Academic, Cultural Arts, and Current Events Reading—Magazines: Airplanes

Students cut pictures of airplanes from magazines and write sentences about what an airplane does and what it can carry.

Examples of vocabulary: *fly, carry people, medicine, mail.*

Patterning—rē

Make words beginning with rē-. Discuss meanings.

Examples: reel, read, return, refrigerator, relax.

Student-Made Material: Given a circular pattern, each student will write rē in the center and endings along the edge, forming new words. Students exchange circles and read each other's words.

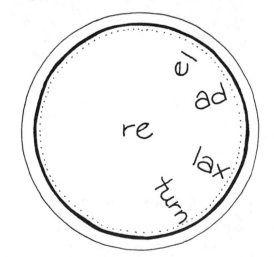

Recreational Reading—Library Books

Find and pronounce words containing v.

LESSON 52

Introductory Phonics/Spelling—C

Discuss the fact that the first word of a sentence is capitalized. Students give sentences beginning with C.

Examples: Come here. Can you see? Chocolate cake is my favorite. Cats are pets.

Review Phonics/Spelling—e, i

Review clusters from earlier lessons. Students give others.

Examples: fried eggs, elm tree, bell rings, ice cream.

Language Experience—Animals: Cats

Students suggest things cats can do. Write them on the board. Students write sentences.

Examples of vocabulary: *meow softly, purr with contentment, fight with dogs, lick their babies.*

Academic, Cultural Arts, and Current Events Reading—Magazines: Airplanes

Students cut pictures of various types of flying machines and other things associated with flying from magazines and label.

Examples: *jet, helicopter, pilot, seat belt.*

Patterning—rī

Introductory device: a toy rifle.
Examples: rice, ride, right, rise, riot.

Student-Made Material: Students work in pairs and form a design using rice, glue, and construction paper.

Recreational Reading—Library Books

Find and pronounce words containing u.

LESSON 53

Introductory Phonics/Spelling—D̲, E̲

Introductory device: Donald Duck. Students give others names or beginnings of sentences with D̲ and E̲.

Examples: D̲isney World; D̲ennis the Menace; "D̲eck the Halls;" E̲aster Bunny; E̲ach day we sing; Lon d̲on, E̲ngland; E̲xit sign.

Review Phonics/Spelling—o̲

Review clusters in Lessons 47 and 50. Students give others.

Examples: go o̲d o̲range, lo̲ud radi o̲, n o̲ thank yo̲u, o̲ld w o̲man.

Language Experience—Animals: Cats

Students draw a picture of a cat. They label its parts and write other words describing it.

Examples of vocabulary: *long tail, soft fur, pointed ears, cuddly kitten.*

Academic, Cultural Arts, and Current Events Reading—Mathematics Textbook: Words for Places

In math book students locate words referring to places.

Patterning—rō

Introductory device: a rose or picture of a rose.
Examples: r o̲ad, r o̲ast, r o̲bot, r o̲ll, r o̲w.

Student-Made Material: Each student draws a robot on a sheet of paper and writes words containing rō on the robot. Students use this material with other students.

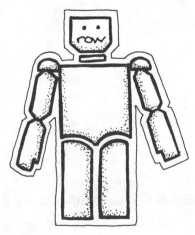

Recreational Reading—Library Books

Find and pronounce words containing u̲.

LESSON 54

Introductory Phonics/Spelling—F

Introductory device: Fred Flintstone.

Examples: Friday morning, Frankenstein the monster, month of February, Frosty the Snowman, Firestone tires.

Review Phonics/Spelling—u, A

Review Lessons 49 and 51.

Examples: in August, Autumn is a season, Ann's umbrella, Andrews Avenue.

Language Experience—Animals: Cats

Students make cat books. Students write a story about their cat and illustrate their books.

Examples of vocabulary: *do tricks, get tangled in yarn, scratch furniture, climb trees.*

Academic, Cultural Arts, and Current Events Reading—Mathematics Textbook: Words for Places

Students locate position words in math textbook. Discuss their importance in problem solving.

Examples: *after, next, between, over.*

Patterning—rū, sū

Introductory devices: ruler, picture of a suit.
Examples: rude, ruby, ruin; sue, super.

Student-Made Material: Students work in groups of three or four and make a magazine picture collage of *super* things.

Recreational Reading—Library Books

Find and pronounce words containing u.

LESSON 55

Introductory Phonics/Spelling—<u>G</u>, <u>H</u>

Introductory device: Read story of *Goldilocks and the Three Bears*.

Examples: Pluto and <u>G</u>oofy, Curious <u>G</u>eorge, <u>G</u>ood Times, <u>H</u>appy Birthday, <u>H</u>alloween night, <u>H</u>elp me.

Review Phonics/Spelling—<u>B</u>

Review Lesson 51. Examples: "<u>B</u>illy <u>B</u>oy," <u>B</u>atman and Robin, <u>B</u> C Powder.

Language Experience—Animals: Horses

Students list things that horses can do. Write on the board. Students write sentences with some.

Examples: *carry people, gallop fast, pull a plow, jump fences.*

Academic, Cultural Arts, and Current Events Reading—Newspaper: <u>X</u>, <u>x</u>

Cut or tear the letters <u>X</u>, <u>x</u> and words containing them from the newspaper.

Patterning—<u>sā</u>

Introduction: Rules of safety.
Examples: <u>sa</u>il, <u>sa</u>cred, <u>sa</u>me, <u>sa</u>ve, <u>sa</u>int.

Student-Made Material: Each group of three or four students draws and/or finds in magazines pictures of safety rules.

Recreational Reading—Library Books

Find and pronounce words containing <u>j</u>.

LESSON 56

Introductory Phonics/Spelling—I

Introductory device: Indian Chief.

Examples: Idaho potatoes, I'm at school, country of Ireland, F. B. I., Interstate 85, Ivory Soap.

Review Phonics/Spelling—C, D

Review Lessons 52 and 53.

Examples: Charlotte's Web, Santa Claus, Dick Van Dyke, handsome Danny.

Language Experience—Animals: Horses

Students draw a picture of a horse and label its parts.

Examples: *long mane, shoed hoof, ears with spots, brown eyes.*

Academic, Cultural Arts, and Current Events Reading—Newspaper: Y, y

Cut or tear the letters Y, y and words containing them from the newspaper.

Patterning—sē

Introduction: Teacher says, "I have a secret beginning with sē." Children suggest words.

Examples: seal, seed, seem, season.

Student-Made Material: Each student uses a needle, thread, and assortment of seeds to make a seed necklace. Other objects (macaroni, buttons) can be added.

Recreational Reading—Library Books

Find and pronounce words containing j.

LESSON 57

Introductory Phonics/Spelling—<u>J</u>, <u>K</u>

Introduction: Read *Jack Sprat*.
Examples: "<u>J</u>ack and <u>J</u>ill," "<u>J</u>ack and the Bean-stalk," Tokyo in <u>J</u>apan, next <u>J</u>anuary, <u>K</u>ing <u>K</u>ong, <u>K</u>ris <u>K</u>ringle, <u>K</u>ent Street, <u>K</u>ittens are tiny.

Review Phonics/Spelling—<u>E</u>

Review Lesson 53.
Examples: <u>E</u>nglish muffins, <u>E</u>ggs taste good. Queen <u>E</u>lizabeth, <u>E</u>skimo igloos.

Academic, Cultural Arts, and Current Events Reading—Magazines: Hair

Cut pictures/words from magazines about hair. Students write a color word beside each.

Patterning—<u>sī</u>, <u>sō</u>

Make words beginning with <u>sī</u> and <u>sō</u>. Discuss meanings.
Examples: <u>si</u>ze, <u>si</u>ren, <u>si</u>lent, <u>so</u>ap, <u>so</u>da, <u>so</u>lo.

Student-Made Material: Each student carves an object from a small piece of *soap* (animals, trees, flowers). (Plastic knives can be used.) Students use this material with other students.

Recreational Reading—Library Books

Find and pronounce words containing <u>j</u>.

LESSON 58

Introductory Phonics/Spelling—<u>L</u>

Introductory device: Liberty Bell.
Examples: <u>L</u>inus and <u>L</u>ucy, <u>L</u>abor Day, pretty <u>L</u>inda, <u>L</u>eo the <u>L</u>ion, <u>L</u>assie, <u>L</u>et me help you.

Review Phonics/Spelling—<u>F</u>, <u>G</u>

Review Lessons 54 and 55.
Examples: Tampa, <u>F</u>lorida, <u>F</u>all is before win-ter, <u>G</u>rand Canyon, <u>G</u>eorge Washington, <u>G</u>et up!

Language Experience—Animals: Cows

Discuss and write sentences about the various things that cows give us.
Examples of vocabulary: *milk and cream, creamy butter, pieces of beef, leather for shoes.*

Academic, Cultural Arts, and Current Events Reading—Magazines: Hair

Cut pictures of hair from magazines. Students write sentences about the pictures found.
Examples: *Her hair is very long. His hair is curly.*

Patterning—ta̅

Read Beatrix Potter's *The Tailor of Gloucester.* Make words with ta̅.
Examples: ta̅ble, ta̅il, ta̅ste, ta̅ilor, ta̅me.

Student-Made Material: Each student cuts a rectangle and two circles from poster board. The two circles are attached by brads to both ends of the rectangle. The letters ta̅ are written on the circle at the left and word endings are written on the circle at the right.

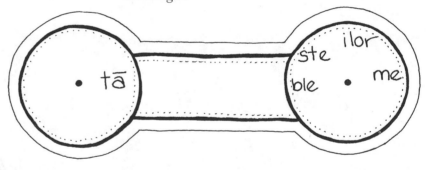

Recreational Reading—Library Books

Find and pronounce words containing k̲.

LESSON 59

Introductory Phonics/Spelling—M̲, N̲

Introductory device: Mickey Mouse.
Examples: planet M̲ars, M̲erry Christmas, M̲ississippi River, M̲ilky Way, M̲cDonald's burgers, N̲orth Pole, N̲ine is a number, my friend N̲ancy, state of N̲evada, N̲estle's chocolate.

Review Phonics/Spelling—H̲

Review Lesson 55.
Examples: H̲appy H̲olidays, H̲olidays are fun, H̲eadless H̲orseman.

Language Experience—Animals: Cows

Post the rhyme, "Hey Diddle Diddle." Class reads. Students draw and label characters. Students find sentence about cow's role by silent reading and write on paper.

Examples of vocabulary: *the cat, his fiddle, dish and spoon, the moon.*

Academic, Cultural Arts, and Current Events Reading—Science Textbook: Word Referring to People

Locate words referring to people. Discuss what each is doing in the context of the material.

Patterning—tē

Introductory device: Indian teepee.
Examples: teach, team, tear, tease, tee.

Student-Made Material: Each student draws a teepee on poster paper and divides it into parts. A word containing tē is written on each part. Students cut teepee apart and put together as a puzzle.

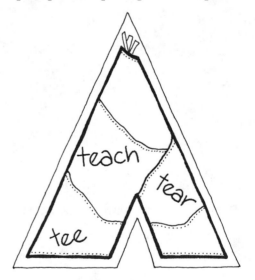

Recreational Reading—Library Books

Find and pronounce words containing k.

LESSON 60

Introductory Phonics/Spelling—<u>O</u>

Introductory device: <u>O</u>live <u>O</u>yl.

Examples: <u>O</u>ctober weather, state of <u>O</u>klahoma, <u>O</u>ctopuses have eight arms, Pacific <u>O</u>cean, <u>O</u>pen the door!

Review Phonics/Spelling—<u>I</u>, <u>J</u>

Review Lessons 56 and 57.

Examples: <u>I</u>talian pizza, <u>I</u>ce Cream store, "<u>J</u>ingle Bells," <u>J</u>une and <u>J</u>uly.

Language Experience—Animals: Cows

Students write stories about cows. Assist in spelling.

Examples of vocabulary: *say moo, eat grass, bulls have horns.*

Academic, Cultural Arts, and Current Events Reading—Science Textbook: Words Referring to People

Locate words used to describe people.

Patterning—t<u>ī</u>

Introductory device: tiger.

Examples: <u>ti</u>de, <u>ti</u>ght, <u>ti</u>me, <u>ti</u>tle, <u>ti</u>re.

Student-Made Material: Each pair of students cuts a circle and a spinner from poster board. Words containing t<u>ī</u> are written around the circle and the spinner is attached with a brad. Students take turns spinning the spinner and making a sentence using the word toward which the spinner is pointed.

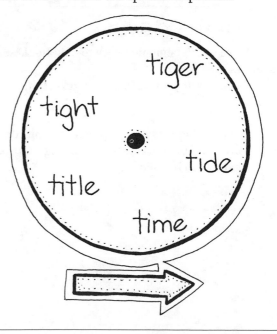

Recreational Reading—Library Books

Find and pronounce words containing k.

LESSON 61

Introductory Phonics/Spelling—P, Qu

Introduction: "Peter Piper."
Examples: Peppermint Patty, Pink Panther, Peter Pan, my sister Polly, Please pass the salt, Quaker Oats, Queen Mary, Quit that! The sign says Quiet.

Review Phonics/Spelling—K

Review Lesson 57.
Examples: Karo Syrup, Kentucky Fried Chicken, King Arthur, Captain Kangaroo.

Language Experience—Animals: Goats

Read or show filmstrip *Three Billy Goats Gruff.* Students draw a picture of the story and write sentences describing their picture.
Examples: *The smallest goat is crossing the bridge. The ogre said, "I'm going to eat you up!"*

Academic, Cultural Arts, and Current Events Reading—Newspaper: Z, z

Cut or tear the letters Z, z and words containing them from the newspaper.

Patterning—tō, tū

Make words beginning with tō- and tū-. Discuss meanings.
Examples: toe, toast, tone, tow, tube, tulip, tune, tuna.

Student-Made Material: Each student draws around his or her big toe and creates a design. Crayons and/or paints can be used.

Recreational Reading—Library Books

Find and pronounce words containing a.

LESSON 62

Introductory Phonics/Spelling—R

Introduction: Read *Little Red Riding Hood*.
Examples: Raggedy Ann, Rip Van Winkle, Read me a story, Rabbits have long ears, my cousin Robert, "Rudolph the Red Nosed Reindeer."

Review Phonics/Spelling—L, M

Review Lessons 58 and 59.
Examples: Los Angeles, Lux dishwashing soap, Speed Limit, Mother's Day, Monday, Mexico is our neighbor.

Language Experience—Animals: Goats

Discuss goats and what they can do.
Examples of vocabulary: *butt with their horns, give milk, eat paper, chase people.*

Academic, Cultural Arts, and Current Events Reading—Newspaper: A, a

Cut or tear the letters A, a and words containing them from the newspaper.

Patterning—vā, vē

Make words beginning with vā and vē. Discuss meanings.
Examples: vase, vacant, vacation, vain, veto, veal, Venus, vehicle.

Student-Made Material: Students work in pairs and unscramble the following words. Encourage students to think of additional words containing vā and vē and see if other members of the class can unscramble them.

evsa	etov
nvtaca	lave
ictnovaa	sneuV
nvia	clhevei

Recreational Reading—Library Books

Find and pronounce words containing a.

Success in Beginning Reading and Writing Lessons

phase 3   lessons 63-90

Beginning with Phase 3, all examples written on the Phonics/Spelling charts are in *sentences* rather than clusters or single words. Examples on the Patterning charts can be single words.

LESSON 63

Introductory Phonics/Spelling—S, T

Introductory device: Superman.
Examples: The devil is sometimes called Satan. Sally is a character in Peanuts. South Carolina is a state. "Three Blind Mice" is a song. I live in Texas. The window is open.

Review Phonics/Spelling—N

Review Lesson 59. Make sentences with some.
Examples: New York is a big city. Nellie is in my class. My birthday is in November.

Language Experience—Animals: Goats

Students write stories about goats. Assist in spelling.
Examples of vocabulary: *nanny goat, kid, hoof, beard.*

Academic, Cultural Arts, and Current Events Reading—Magazines: Toys

Students cut out pictures of toys they would like to give to their friends. They write sentences about each telling why they chose it.
Examples: *Mary likes to play with dolls. Jim collects little cars.*

142

Patterning—v̄ī, v̄ō

Introductory device: Hang words on a vine.
Examples: violin, violet, Viceroy, vitamin, vote, volt, vocal, vocabulary.

Student-Made Material: Each student covers a sheet of thick paper with patches of different colors of wax crayons. A black crayon is then used to cover the other colors. A violet is scratched on the paper by using a toothpick or prongs of a fork.

Recreational Reading—Library Books

Find and pronounce words containing a.

LESSON 64

Introductory Phonics/Spelling—U

Introductory device: Map of U.S.
Examples: We live in the United States. Umbrellas are for rainy days. Uncle Bob lives on a farm. My sister goes to State University.

Review Phonics/Spelling—O, P

Review Lessons 60 and 61. Make sentences with some.
Examples: Mrs. O'Neal is my teacher. I read a story about Ollie. Put your book away. I live on Pearson Street.

Language Experience—Cartoons

Students draw picture of favorite cartoon character and write a description of the character.
Examples of vocabulary: *eats spinach, very strong, can fly fast, x-ray vision.*

Academic, Cultural Arts, and Current Events Reading—Magazines: Feelings

Students cut or tear pictures of happy people from magazines and write a sentence explaining why they are happy.

143

Patterning—wā

Discuss the meanings of waist and waste. Make other words that begin with wā.

Examples: wade, waitress, wake, wave, way.

Student-Made Material: Each student writes the letters of the alphabet on paper and then cuts them apart. Students work in groups of three or four and form as many words as they can containing wā using the alphabet letters they have written. The words can be glued on construction paper.

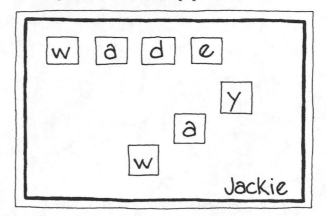

Recreational Reading—Library Books

Find and pronounce words containing c.

LESSON 65

Introductory Phonics/Spelling—V, W

Make sentences containing words with V and W.

Examples: Venus is a planet. Violets are purple. Send cards on Valentine's Day. Watermelon is my favorite fruit. Our capital is Washington, D.C. Tomorrow is Wednesday.

Review Phonics/Spelling—Qu

Review Lesson 61. Make sentences with some.

Examples: John Quincy Adams was a president. San Quentin is a prison. Have you ever been to Quebec?

Language Experience—Cartoons

Students cut out or draw a cartoon and write about it.

Examples of vocabulary: *fat man, eat the cake, funny, in trouble.*

Academic, Cultural Arts, and Current Events Reading—Social Studies Textbook: Important Words in Chapter Titles

Students locate and discuss the meanings of important words in chapter titles. Call attention to the capital letters.

Patterning—wē

Introduction: Discuss what a week is and show how it is indicated on a calendar.

Examples: weak, weed, wee, weep, weave.

Student-Made Material: Each student will create a paper-weaving design. Cut a series of slits in a piece of construction paper, making sure there is a border on each side. Cut strips of colored paper, magazines, or wallpaper. These strips are woven through the slits in the paper.

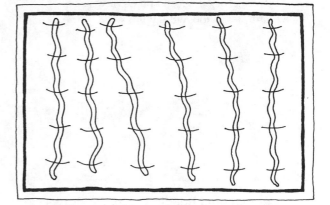

Recreational Reading—Library Books

Find and pronounce words containing c.

LESSON 66

Introductory Phonics/Spelling—X, Y, Z

Make sentences containing X, Y, and Z.

Examples: Christmas is sometimes written Xmas. X-ray his arm, Nurse. I go swimming at the YMCA. Yo-yos are fun to play with. Zebras have black and white stripes. Always use your Zip Code.

Review Phonics/Spelling—R

Review Lesson 62. Make sentences with some.

Examples: Raymond lives next door. Records are round.

Language Experience—Cartoons

Students write a story about a *cartoon* they saw on television.
Examples of vocabulary: *chased the mouse, saved the girl, a big monster, on his dog house.*

Academic, Cultural Arts, and Current Events Reading—Social Studies Textbook: Important Words in Chapter Titles

Students locate in the chapter words that are found in the title. Discuss the purpose of chapter titles.

Patterning—wī

Introductory device: a piece of wire.
Examples: wide, wife, wild, wind, wipe.

Student-Made Material: Each student copies the following sentences and places one of the words from the list in each sentence. Sentences are then read to another member of the class.

If you spill your milk _____ it up.

The road is _____ enough for the big truck to get through.

We will _____ up the clock.

The lion is a _____ animal.

Use the _____ to hold the objects together.

Recreational Reading—Library Books

Find and pronounce words containing c.

LESSON 67

Introductory Phonics/Spelling—br

Introductory device: brick.
Examples: That brave boy used his brain. The witch said, "Abracadabra," and was off on her broomstick. Bring me the other brand of broccoli. Please brush your brother's brown hair.

Review Phonics/Spelling—S, T

Review Lesson 63.
Further examples: Smoking is bad for you. We have a Siamese cat. Teddy bears are nice to sleep with. My neighbor is Mr. Thomas.

Language Experience—Television Program

Students write about a television program that is not a cartoon.
Examples of vocabulary: *cowboys, fighting, detective, school.*

Academic, Cultural Arts, and Current Events Reading—Newspaper: E̲, e̲

Cut or tear the letters E̲, e̲ and words containing them from the newspaper.

Patterning—wō, yō

Make words beginning with wō and yō. Discuss meanings.

Examples: wo̲n't, wo̲e, yo̲-yo, yo̲gurt, yo̲lk.

Student-Made Material: Each student will create an object containing wō or yō using drinking straws. Students make an outline of the drawing (yo-yo) on cardboard. They cut straws into small pieces and place them in a box. Students then glue straw pieces perpendicularly to the cardboard.

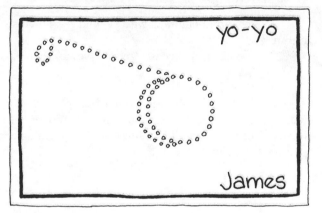

Recreational Reading—Library Books

Find and pronounce words containing i̲.

LESSON 68

Introductory Phonics/Spelling—bl̲

Introductory device: blue objects.

Examples: If air bl̲ows into your eyes, you will bl̲ink. The bl̲aze will bl̲ister your hand. Don't bl̲ame anyone for the accident. If you cut yourself, you will bl̲eed.

Review Phonics/Spelling—U̲

Review Lesson 64.

Examples: U̲se soap on those hands! We saw a U̲.F.O. *The U̲gly Duckling* is one of my favorite stories.

Language Experience—Television Program: Happy

Students draw a picture of a scene from a happy television program and write about it.

Examples of vocabulary: *visit, saved, jokes, crazy.*

Academic, Cultural Arts, and Current Events Reading—Newspapers: I, i

Cut or tear the letters I, i and words containing them from the newspaper.

Patterning—yē, zē

Make words beginning with yē- and zē-. Discuss meanings.

Examples: year, yeast, zebra, New Zealand, zero.

Student-Made Material: Each pair of students will think of a sentence containing zē and/or yē words. This sentence will be illustrated by forming a picture from felt.

Recreational Reading—Library Books

Find and pronounce words containing i.

LESSON 69

Introductory Phonics/Spelling—cr, dr

Introductory device: crown/dress.
Examples: The crocodile crossed the creek. Want some ice cream? The baby has a cradle and a crib. Please dry the dishes in the drain. I dreamed I was a princess. The draft is blowing the drapery.

Review Phonics/Spelling—V

Review Lesson 65.
Examples: My mother's name is Vicky. Violins make pretty music. Vegetables are good for you.

Language Experience—Television Program: News

Discuss the divisions of a news program: news, sports, weather. Each child chooses one area and writes about it.

Academic, Cultural Arts, and Current Events Reading—Magazines: Children

Cut pictures of children from magazines. Students write sentences describing the pictures.

Patterning—er, ir, ur

Make words containing er, ir, and ur. Discuss meanings.
Examples: paper, bird, turn, super, first, curl.

Student-Made Material: Each student is given the star pattern and writes a word containing er, ir, or ur in each section. The star is cut apart and given to a partner who puts the star together by pronouncing each word.

Recreational Reading—Library Books

Find and pronounce words containing <u>i</u>.

LESSON 70

Introductory Phonics/Spelling—<u>fl</u>

Introductory device: <u>fl</u>owers.
Examples: The <u>fl</u>ag is <u>fl</u>ying in the wind. Can you do a <u>fl</u>ip? We saw a <u>fl</u>ock of ducks <u>fl</u>oating on the river. The <u>fl</u>ame <u>fl</u>ashed light all around.

Review Phonics/Spelling—<u>W</u>, <u>br</u>

Review Lessons 65 and 67.
Examples: <u>W</u>hy did you <u>br</u>eak the <u>br</u>acelet? That <u>br</u>at's name is <u>W</u>illiam. <u>W</u>inter is the coldest season. <u>W</u>ilbur climbed to the highest <u>br</u>anch.

Language Experience—People at School

Students draw a picture of their teacher and write about him or her.
Examples of vocabulary: *very nice, makes me work hard, handsome, reads us stories.*

Academic, Cultural Arts, and Current Events Reading—Magazines: Children

Cut pictures of children doing things from magazines. Students write sentences telling what each child is doing.

Patterning—<u>er</u>, <u>ir</u>, <u>ur</u>

Make words containing <u>er</u>, <u>ir</u>, and <u>ur</u>. Discuss meanings.
Examples: h<u>ur</u>t, sp<u>ur</u>t, st<u>ir</u>, sh<u>ir</u>t, moth<u>er</u>, h<u>er</u>.

Student-Made Material: Each student will form an object containing <u>er</u>, <u>ir</u> or <u>ur</u> by using toothpicks. Toothpicks can be glued together to form three-dimensional structures, then glued on paper.

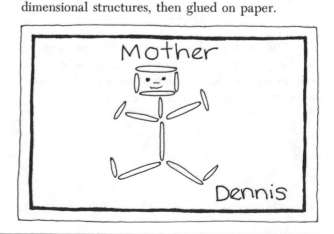

Recreational Reading—Library Books

Find and pronounce words containing h.

LESSON 71

Introductory Phonics/Spelling—fr, gr

Introductory device: a green frog.
Examples: Grace has freckles. Grandmother serves us potatoes and gravy. I mowed the grass in the front yard. He frowned when he saw his grade. France is a great country. The picture has a gray frame.

Review Phonics/Spelling—X, Y

Review Lesson 66.
Examples: You need to put an X if it's wrong. Size XL is very large. Yellow is a color. New Year's Day is January 1.

Language Experience—People at School

Students choose one friend in the classroom and describe him or her.
Examples of vocabulary: *bigger than me, wears glasses, curly hair, reads well.*

Academic, Cultural Arts, and Current Events Reading—Mathematics Textbook: Words for Objects

Find and list on the board words in the math textbook that represent objects.

Patterning—or

Introductory device: fork.
Examples: north, order, fort, Ford, corduroy.

Student-Made Material: Each group of three or four students draws a picture of a large fork on a piece of paper. The group then thinks of as many uses of a fork as possible within a given amount of time. These ideas can be written on the fork and shared with the class.

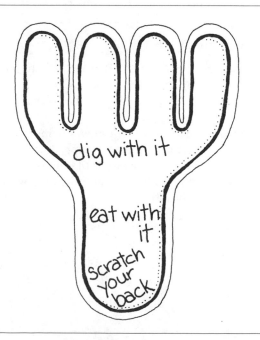

Recreational Reading—Library Books

Find and pronounce words containing h.

LESSON 72

Introductory Phonics/Spelling—gl, pl

Introductory device: piece of glass and plastic.
Examples: The planet Pluto glitters like a star.
I am glad Gladys could come. Glue the airplane picture on your paper. Please serve your plate. The globe is a model of the earth. Water the plants.

Review Phonics/Spelling—Z

Review Lesson 66.
Examples: Zero means nothing. Zoos are where many animals can be seen. Go slowly when you see a School Zone sign.

Language Experience—People at School

Discuss various people who work in a school and their jobs. Students write about one of their choice.
Examples of vocabulary: *answers the phone, is the boss, fixes things, cooks the lunches.*

Academic, Cultural Arts, and Current Events Reading—Mathematics Textbook: Words for Objects

Find words for objects in the math textbook. List on the board. Students give a word that describes each object.

Patterning—dy

Introductory device: Raggedy Andy. Make words containing dy. Discuss meanings.
Examples: handy, shady, ready, baldy.

Student-Made Material: Each group of three or four students divides a piece of paper into four sections and writes the key word at the top of each section. Each group will list as many rhyming words of the key word as possible.

shady	baldy	ready	handy

Fred   Roberta   Clare

Recreational Reading—Library Books

Find and pronounce words containing <u>h</u>.

LESSON 73

Introductory Phonics/Spelling—<u>pr</u>, <u>sm</u>

Introductory device: picture of the president smiling.

Examples: What is the <u>pr</u>ice of a <u>pr</u>etzel? You must be <u>sm</u>art to win the <u>pr</u>ize. Does a <u>pr</u>une <u>sm</u>ell? <u>Sm</u>oking can cause health <u>pr</u>oblems. Use soap or the <u>sm</u>udge will just <u>sm</u>ear. Mr. <u>Sm</u>ith is a <u>pr</u>inter.

Review Phonics/Spelling—<u>bl</u>

Review Lesson 68.

Examples: The <u>bl</u>anket will keep you warm. I carved a boat from the <u>bl</u>ock of wood. A person who cannot see is <u>bl</u>ind.

Language Experience—Places at School

Students write a description of their classroom.
Examples of vocabulary: *many desks, library books, blackboard, coat closets.*

Academic, Cultural Arts, and Current Events Reading—Newspapers: <u>O</u>, <u>o</u>

Cut or tear the letters <u>O</u>, <u>o</u> and words containing them from the newspaper.

Patterning—<u>oo</u>, <u>ew</u>

Introduction: Discuss the moon.
Examples: z<u>oo</u>, bl<u>ew</u>, gr<u>ew</u>, s<u>oo</u>n, f<u>oo</u>d, t<u>oo</u>th.

Student-Made Material: Each student selects a word card containing <u>oo</u> or <u>ew</u> and pantomimes the word. Allow each student an opportunity to pantomime his or her word.

Recreational Reading—Library Books

Find and pronounce words containing t.

LESSON 74

Introductory Phonics/Spelling—sl, tr

Introductory device: a treasure chest.
Examples: We slept on the train. My sled makes tracks on the snow. I have trouble walking on the slippery ice. Trust me to tell the truth. Try not to slam the door. Slice the meat.

Review Phonics/Spelling—cr

Review Lesson 69.
Examples: A crow is a black bird. The crackers are crisp. We saw a crab crawl across the sand.

Language Experience—Places at School

Students write about the library and their visits there.
Examples of vocabulary: *librarian, check out, easy books, tables and chairs*.

Academic, Cultural Arts, and Current Events Reading—Newspaper: U, u

Cut or tear the letters U, u and words containing them from the newspaper.

Patterning—ss

Introductory device: picture of Lassie. Discuss single sound made by ss.
Examples: grass, miss, moss, press, Russell, professor.

Student-Made Material: Each student creates a sponge print by *pressing* pieces of sponge onto paper. Use tempera paint and dip pieces of sponges into the paint. Press lightly onto the paper.

Recreational Reading—Library Books

Find and pronounce words containing t.

LESSON 75

Introductory Phonics/Spelling—sc, scr

Introductory device: scarf/screw.

Examples: What score did Scott make? I want to be a Boy Scout. Do you like butterscotch candy? The baby scribbled on the wall. There is a hole in the screen. The little girl screamed when she scratched her leg.

Review Phonics/Spelling—dr

Review Lesson 69.

Examples: Did you drop your drawing? He plays the drum in the band. I wish the faucet would not drip.

Language Experience—Places at School

Students write about the cafeteria or other special purpose place within the school.

Examples of vocabulary: *stand in line, pay the lady, long tables, take our trays.*

Academic, Cultural Arts, and Current Events Reading—Magazines: Cars

Students cut a picture of a car from a magazine and describe it.

Patterning—oi, oy

Introductory device: picture of a boy.
Examples: toy, soil, enjoy, destroy, boil, spoil.

Student-Made Material: Each student draws a picture of a boy on a piece of paper and writes words containing oy and oi on the boy. With a partner, words are pronounced and sentences given using the words.

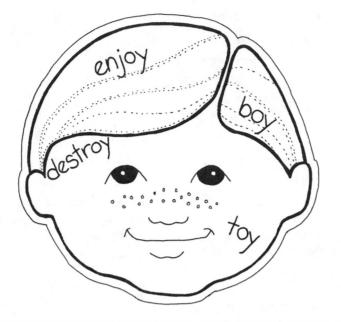

Recreational Reading—Library Books

Find and pronounce words containing <u>t</u>.

LESSON 76

Introductory Phonics/Spelling—<u>sp</u>, <u>spl</u>

Introductory device: a spider
Examples: The <u>sp</u>y is from <u>Sp</u>ain. The President made a <u>sp</u>eech. The drink you <u>sp</u>illed left a <u>sp</u>ot on your shirt. It is fun to <u>spl</u>ash in the water. I have a <u>spl</u>inter in my finger. Want a banana <u>spl</u>it?

Review Phonics/Spelling—<u>fl</u>

Review Lesson 70.
Examples: Mother just mopped the <u>fl</u>oor. Do you like corn <u>fl</u>akes? Birds <u>fl</u>ap their wings when they <u>fl</u>y.

Language Experience—Places to Go

Students discuss and write about places they can get to by walking.
Examples of vocabulary: *friend's house, playground, secret hiding place, the store.*

Academic, Cultural Arts, and Current Events Reading—Magazines: Cars

Students find pictures and label parts of cars. Examples: *tires, engine, window, lights.*

Patterning—ll

Introductory device: ball. Discuss single sound made by ll.

Examples: ta<u>ll</u>, i<u>ll</u>, thri<u>ll</u>, spe<u>ll</u>, do<u>ll</u>, sha<u>ll</u>.

Student-Made Material: Each pair of students looks through magazines and finds words and/or pictures containing ll. These are glued on construction paper. Students can write sentences containing the words found in the magazines.

Recreational Reading—Library Books

Find words at the beginnings of sentences.

LESSON 77

Introductory Phonics/Spelling—st, str

Introductory device: a stamp.

Examples: <u>St</u>op that thief! It is fun to throw <u>st</u>ones in a <u>st</u>ream. <u>Str</u>ing is not as <u>str</u>ong as <u>st</u>eel. The <u>str</u>awberries are by the <u>st</u>ove. Look before you <u>st</u>art to cross the <u>str</u>eet. Who is that <u>str</u>anger?

Review Phonics/Spelling—fr

Review Lesson 71.

Examples: The present is from <u>Fr</u>ed. One piece of <u>fr</u>uit is <u>fr</u>ee. <u>Fr</u>ank is my best <u>fr</u>iend.

Language Experience—Places to Go

Students discuss and write about places one goes in a car.

Examples: *Grandmother's house, grocery store, out shopping, on trips.*

**Academic, Cultural Arts, and Current
Events Reading—Science Textbook:
Words that Describe**

Locate words in science textbook that describe things. Discuss what they describe. Substitute other descriptive words and discuss the change in meaning.

Patterning—al, all

Introduction: Determine who are the tallest and smallest persons in the class.

Examples: fall, ball, final, mall, spinal, already.

Student-Made Material: Each student creates a rhyming tree. On the left side of the tree words containing al and all are written. On the right side a rhyming word is written. (Note: Rhyming words can be nonsense words.)

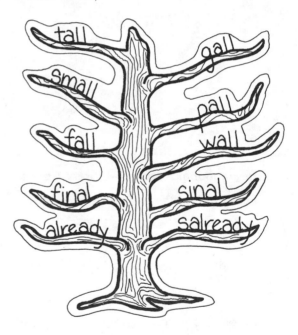

Recreational Reading—Library Books

Find and pronounce words ending in -ing and -ed.

LESSON 78

Introductory Phonics/Spelling—sk, sn

Introductory device: skunk/snake.

Examples: I like your skirt. A skull on a bottle means it is poisonous. Have you ever been snow skiing

Review Phonics/Spelling—gr

Review Lesson 71.

Examples: My family went to the Grand Canyon. Try to grab the ball. A grain of sand is very small.

or ice skating? Another word for a frying pan is a
skillet. When you have a cold you sneeze and sniffle.
My daddy snores when he takes a snooze.

Language Experience—Places to Go

Discuss and write about places far away to which one has to fly in
an airplane or go by boat.
Examples: *Yellowstone National Park, England, Atlantic Ocean, seat
belt.*

Academic, Cultural Arts, and Current Events Reading—Science Textbook: Words that Describe

Locate and discuss words in science textbook that describe things. Try
to think of another descriptive word that means the same thing; the opposite.

Patterning—au, aw

Introductory device: a straw.
Examples: thaw, taught, caught, yawn, draw.

Student-Made Material: Each group of three or
four students thinks of a way to use a *straw*. This
way is written on a piece of paper and one member
of each group pantomimes a way a straw can be used.

I can look through a straw.

Recreational Reading—Library Books

Find and pronounce short words.

LESSON 79

Introductory Phonics/Spelling—sh, shr

Introductory device: shoe.
Examples: Daddy shaves with a sharp razor. Show me the old shack. We went shopping for a new shirt. I like to eat fried shrimp. I get to help plant the shrubs. My sweater has shrunk.

Review Phonics/Spelling—gl

Review Lesson 72.
Examples: What a gloomy day! Did you get a glimpse of Santa? Eagles can glide through the air.

Language Experience—Games

Students discuss and write about a game they like to play with other people.
Examples of vocabulary: *tag base, roll the dice, captain of the team, let's pretend.*

Academic, Cultural Arts, and Current Events Reading—Newspaper: Sight Words

Find these words in the newspaper and cut them out: *and, the, for, why, which, you.*

Patterning—un

Make words containing un.
Examples: fun, under, until, sunny, undone.

Student-Made Material: Each group of three or four students writes a story using as many words containing un as possible. Each group's story is shared with the class.
Example: We had fun until it started raining. The sunny weather hid under the cloud.

Recreational Reading—Library Books

Find and pronounce long words.

LESSON 80

Introductory Phonics/Spelling—ch

Introductory device: picture of children.
Examples: When you have an itch, you usually scratch it. Count your change. We have a charge account. It is chilly outside.

Review Phonics/Spelling—pl

Review Lesson 72.
Examples: I like your plaid shirt. What is two plus three? We need pliers to loosen that nut.

Language Experience—Games

Students discuss and write about games that can be played alone.
Examples of vocabulary: *dolls, carpenter, puzzles, imaginary.*

Academic, Cultural Arts, and Current Events Reading—Newspaper: Sight Words

Find these words in the newspaper and cut them out: *when, friend, your, to, some, should.*

Patterning—<u>oo</u>, <u>u</u>

Make words containing the sound in *book* and *push.*
Examples: l<u>oo</u>k, p<u>u</u>ll, c<u>oo</u>k, h<u>oo</u>d, p<u>u</u>t.

Student-Made Material: Each student creates a miniature book consisting of words containing <u>oo</u> and <u>u</u>. Pieces of construction paper can be stapled together and the words can be cut from magazines and newspapers and glued in the book.

Recreational Reading—Library Books

Find and pronounce words that are the names of things.

LESSON 81

Introductory Phonics/Spelling—<u>th</u>, <u>thr</u>

Introductory device: three thimbles.
Examples: <u>Th</u>under scares me. <u>Th</u>row me <u>th</u>e ball. He ran <u>thr</u>ough <u>th</u>e room.

Review Phonics/Spelling—<u>pr</u>

Review Lesson 73.
Examples: You will need a screwdriver to <u>pr</u>y the top off. A <u>pr</u>ince is the son of a king. What is your favorite TV <u>pr</u>ogram?

Language Experience—Games

Students write about a new game they have learned to play. They may want to write the directions for someone who wants to learn.

161

**Academic, Cultural Arts, and Current
Events Reading—Magazines: Pictures
and Words with the r sound**

Students find pictures of items and words containing the r sound.

Patterning—ble

Introductory device: a table.
Examples: terrible, able, marble, trouble.

Student-Made Material: Each student traces the outline of a cat and cuts slots for a strip of paper to fit through. Beginnings of words ending in -ble are written on the cat. As the strip slides through the slots, new words are formed. Students read their words to a partner.

Recreational Reading—Library Books

Find and pronounce the name of a young person.

LESSON 82

Introductory Phonics/Spelling—qu, squ

Introductory device: a picture of a queen.
Examples: The squash costs a quarter. The squirrel ran up the tree quickly. I have a quilt on my bed. Squat and be very quiet. How did you do on the quiz? A square has four equal sides.

Review Phonics/Spelling—sm

Review Lesson 73.
Examples: An ant is a small animal. The glass is smooth. He smacked her on the cheek.

Language Experience—Toys

Discuss toys that move. Class compiles a list. Each student writes a description of one toy from the list.

Examples of vocabulary: *roller skates, race cars, trucks, bicycles.*

Academic, Cultural Arts, and Current Events Reading—Magazines: Pictures and Words with the r Sound

Students find pictures of items and words containing the r sound.

Patterning—ou, ow

Make words containing the sound in *sound* and *cow.*

Examples: h<u>ou</u>nd, gr<u>ou</u>nd, h<u>ow</u>, pl<u>ow</u>.

Student-Made Material: Each student draws a house and a ladder beside the house. A word containing <u>ou</u> or <u>ow</u> is written on each rung of the ladder. Each student asks a partner to climb the ladder by pronouncing each word.

Recreational Reading—Library Books

Find and pronounce the name of an adult.

LESSON 83

Introductory Phonics/Spelling—sw, wh

Introductory device: sweater.

Examples: <u>Wh</u>en did you get the <u>sw</u>ings? <u>Wh</u>ich baseball cards to you want to <u>sw</u>ap? <u>Wh</u>ich one of

Review Phonics/Spelling—sl

Review Lesson 74.

Examples: Take up the <u>sl</u>ack in the rope. There is a <u>sl</u>ug on the sidewalk. My arm is in a <u>sl</u>ing.

you will sweep the sidewalk? You swim while I lie in
the sun. I've switched to the new wheat cereal.

Language Experience—Toys

Discuss and compile a list of toys that are carried. Each student writes
about one.
Examples of vocabulary: *baby doll, teddy bear, baseball glove, guns.*

Academic, Cultural Arts, and Current
Events Reading—Social Studies Textbook:
Index

Locate words in the index of a social studies textbook and find them
on the pages indicated.

Patterning—pp

Introductory device: an apple.
Examples: slippery, happy, hopping, dripping.

Student-Made Material: Using aluminum foil,
each student creates a foil sculpture of an object
the name of which contains pp.

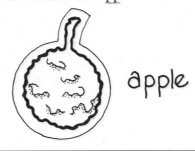

Recreational Reading—Library Books

Find and pronounce words that describe people.

LESSON 84

Introductory Phonics/Spelling—ph

Introductory device: elephant.
Examples: The telephone is ringing. The Phan-
tom is a cartoon strip. We learn sounds letters make in
our phonics lessons. This is a photograph of my
parents.

Review Phonics/Spelling—tr

Review Lesson 74.
Examples: My sister has a tricycle. Let's climb
that tree. I would like a triple dip ice cream cone.

Language Experience—Toys

Discuss and write about toys that remain still.
Examples of vocabulary: *china dogs, play horses, stuffed animals, little animals.*

Academic, Cultural Arts, and Current Events Reading—Social Studies Textbook: Index

Locate words in the index of a social studies textbook and find them on the pages indicated.

Patterning—en, ed

Make words containing en and ed.
Examples: sp**en**d, **en**d, dream**ed**, lov**ed**.

Student-Made Material: Two students work together. One student draws a picture of the beginning of something he or she has dreamed about. The other student draws the ending to this dream. "Dreams" are shared with other members of the class.

Recreational Reading—Library Books

Find and pronounce words that describe animals.

LESSON 85

Introductory Phonics/Spelling—<u>wr</u>

Introductory device: wrench.
Examples: A <u>wr</u>en is a small brown bird. The package is <u>wr</u>apped in red paper. We had a <u>wr</u>eck last week. <u>Wr</u>ite your name on your paper.

Review Phonics/Spelling—<u>scr</u>

Review Lesson 75.
Examples: I had <u>scr</u>ambled eggs for breakfast. Feed the dog the table <u>scr</u>aps. <u>Scr</u>ub your hands.

Language Experience—Clothes

Discuss and write about clothes worn in the winter.
Examples of vocabulary: *sweater, heavy coat, wool pants, jacket.*

Academic, Cultural Arts, and Current Events Reading—Newspaper: Television Guide

Circle words known in the television section of the newspaper.

Patterning—<u>ar</u>

Introductory device: a star.
Examples: c<u>ar</u>, f<u>ar</u>m, b<u>ar</u>n, h<u>ar</u>m, t<u>ar</u>.

Student-Made Material: Each student writes words containing <u>ar</u> on a paper plate. With a partner, words are pronounced and a sentence is given. A hole can be punched in the paper plate and a string put through the hole to make a necklace.

Recreational Reading—Library Books

Find and pronounce action words.

LESSON 86

Introductory Phonics/Spelling—dge, tch

Introductory device: picture of a bridge.
Examples: Let's play dodge ball. Dad has a hunting lodge. A witch rides on a broom. Who is going to be pitcher? Catch the football. This fudge is great.

Review Phonics/Spelling—sc

Review Lesson 75.
Examples: a fish has scales. I have a scar on my leg. Your clothes are scattered all over your room.

Language Experience—Clothes

Discuss and write about clothes worn in the summer.
Examples of vocabulary: *bathing suit, shorts, T-shirts, sandals.*

Academic, Cultural Arts, and Current Events Reading—Newspaper: Television Guide

Find times and channels for television programs.

Patterning—gn, kn

Introductory device: knee.
Examples: gnat, gnaw, sign, know, knot, knock.

knee
gnat
gnaw
sign
know
knot
knock

Student-Made Material: Each student copies the following sentences and words. String is glued from the sentence to the word that completes that sentence. Sentences are read to a partner.

I _____ my address.

Your _____ is bleeding.

Did a _____ bite you?

The dog will _____ the bone.

_____ before you enter.

Can you read the _____?

My head has a _____ on it.

Recreational Reading—Library Books

Find and pronounce happy words.

LESSON 87

Introductory Phonics/Spelling—<u>nd</u>, <u>gh</u>

Introductory device: hand.

Examples: He looks tou<u>gh</u>, but he's very ki<u>nd</u>. I fou<u>nd</u> my shoes u<u>nd</u>er the bed. Dogs have front and hi<u>nd</u> legs. That's a bad cou<u>gh</u>. The po<u>nd</u> is not deep enou<u>gh</u> for the boat. That is the e<u>nd</u>.

Review Phonics/Spelling—<u>spl</u>

Review Lesson 76.

Examples: The egg <u>spl</u>attered on the floor. You did a <u>spl</u>endid job. Let's <u>spl</u>urge and have a milkshake.

Language Experience—Clothes

Discuss clothes worn in special weather. Students describe a special outfit.

Examples of vocabulary: *raincoat, snowsuit, mittens, rubber boots.*

Academic, Cultural Arts, and Current Events Reading—Magazines: <u>d</u> sound

Find pictures of words containing the <u>d</u> sound. Label.

Patterning—<u>mp</u>

Introduction: jump.

Examples: hu<u>mp</u>, sta<u>mp</u>, si<u>mp</u>le, clu<u>mp</u>, stu<u>mp</u>.

Student-Made Material: Each student makes a stamp print. Coat a piece of string with glue and wrap it around a wooden block to form a design. Place a small amount of tempera paint on a piece of scrap paper and smooth it with a brush. Dip the block in the film of paint and press it against a piece of paper.

Recreational Reading—Library Books

Find and pronounce sad words.

LESSON 88

Introductory Phonics/Spelling—<u>ng</u>, <u>ing</u>

Discuss the suffix -ing. Add it to several verbs. Make words with -ng.

Examples: The bird is sing<u>ing</u>. The children are play<u>ing</u>. He is runn<u>ing</u> fast. We learned a new so<u>ng</u> and sa<u>ng</u> it for the others. The bell just ra<u>ng</u>. What is that thi<u>ng</u>?

Review Phonics/Spelling—<u>sp</u>

Review Lesson 76.

Examples: An astronaut goes into <u>sp</u>ace. I'll be glad when <u>sp</u>ring comes. My favorite <u>sp</u>ort is football.

Language Experience—School

Students write about what they have learned in arithmetic.
Examples of vocabulary: *add, subtract, count to one hundred, take away.*

Academic, Cultural Arts, and Current Events Reading—Magazines: <u>d</u> Sound

Find words containing the <u>d</u> sound. Illustrate.

Patterning—<u>ly</u>

Make words containing <u>ly</u>. Discuss meanings.
Examples: kind<u>ly</u>, friend<u>ly</u>, happi<u>ly</u>, smel<u>ly</u>, ug<u>ly</u>.

Student-Made Material: Each student draws a mouse as quietly as possible and writes words containing <u>ly</u> on the mouse. Words are pronounced to a partner.

Recreational Reading—Library Books

Find and pronounce words for buildings.

LESSON 89

Introductory Phonics/Spelling—ck

Introductory device: check mark.
Examples: I bought a pa<u>ck</u>age of chi<u>ck</u>en. Pi<u>ck</u> up your so<u>ck</u>s. Want a li<u>ck</u> of my lollipop? I'm afraid Billy is too si<u>ck</u> to play.

Review Phonics/Spelling—str

Review Lesson 77.
Examples: <u>Str</u>ike three, you're out. Drink your milk with a <u>str</u>aw. I broke the <u>str</u>ap on my book bag.

Language Experience—School

Students discuss and write about what they should do at school.
Examples of vocabulary: *think, do my work, write sentences, behave.*

Academic, Cultural Arts, and Current Events Reading—Mathematics Textbook: Symbols

Locate and discuss the meanings of the mathematical symbols found in math textbooks. Students practice writing the symbols.

Patterning—n't

Discuss contractions made with *not.* Talk about the missing letter and apostrophe.
Examples: ca<u>n't</u>, did<u>n't</u>, should<u>n't</u>, wo<u>n't</u>.

Student-Made Material: Each student writes contractions on one set of cards and the two words the contractions mean on another set of cards. Students trade cards with a partner and match them.

Recreational Reading—Library Books

Find and read sentences about a person.

LESSON 90

Introductory Phonics/Spelling—cl

Introductory device: clown.
Examples: Birds have claws. Look at the pretty clouds. I made a rabbit out of clay. He climbed up that cliff.

Review Phonics/Spelling—st

Review Lesson 77.
Examples: My room is upstairs. Let's stand out here and look at the stars. The story is about a stubborn mule.

Language Experience—School

Students write about what they should not do at school.
Examples of vocabulary: *run in the halls, daydream, fight, pick on others.*

171

Academic, Cultural Arts, and Current Events Reading—Mathematics Textbook: Symbols

Students write symbols found in math textbooks and label each according to its meaning.

Patterning—<u>tion</u>, <u>sion</u>

Make words that contain -<u>tion</u> and -<u>sion</u>.
Examples: addi<u>tion</u>, subtrac<u>tion</u>, televi<u>sion</u>, mi<u>ssion</u>.

Student-Made Material: Each student makes two footballs out of construction paper. Two slots are cut in the footballs and strips of paper are cut that will slide through the slots. Students write -<u>tion</u> on one football and -<u>sion</u> on the other. Word beginnings are written on the strips of paper so that when they are pushed through the slots, new words are formed.

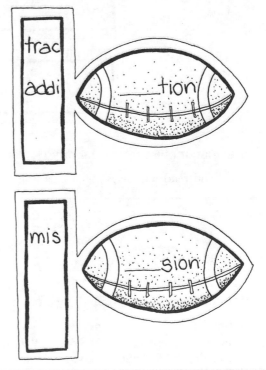

Recreational Reading—Library Books

Find and read sentences about a place.

Success in Beginning Reading and Writing Lessons

phase 4   lessons 91-174

The basic format of Lessons 1–90 is continued for the Phonics/Spelling Modules; however, beginning with Lesson 91 emphasis is placed on syllabication. Each of the Phonics/Spelling Modules contains the suggested letter cluster and syllabication emphasis and two examples of words. The Academic, Cultural Arts, and Current Events Reading Modules contain the suggested material, content-area emphasis, and a guide for asking comprehension questions.

LESSON	PHONICS/STRUCTURAL ANALYSIS	LANGUAGE EXPERIENCE	ACADEMIC, CULTURAL ARTS AND CURRENT EVENTS READING (Materials, Content Emphasis, and Guide for Comprehension)	RECREATIONAL READING
91	2-syllable words: sk skating basket	No theme, story writing	Newspapers, photograph captions Who is in the photograph?	See Chapter Eight
92	2-syllable words: sn unsnarl sneakers	No theme, story writing	Newspapers, photograph captions Why is the photograph important?	See Chapter Eight
93	2-syllable words: sh shaver showroom	No theme, story writing	Newspapers, sports story What happened in the sport story?	See Chapter Eight
94	2-syllable words: ch chunky chicken	No theme, story writing	Newspapers, sports story When did the events take place?	See Chapter Eight
95	2-syllable words: th thimble thunder	No theme, story writing	Catalogues, toy advertisements How are toys used?	See Chapter Eight
96	2-syllable words: qu quiet question	No theme, story writing	Newspapers, front page news story When did an event happen?	See Chapter Eight
97	2-syllable words: squ squander squarely	No theme, story writing	Newspapers, photograph captions What is in the photograph?	See Chapter Eight
98	2-syllable words: sw sweetly swinging	No theme, story writing	Newspapers, front page news story Who is in one article?	See Chapter Eight
99	2-syllable words: wh whimper whisper	No theme, story writing	Catalogues, furniture advertisements What furniture is for sale?	See Chapter Eight
100	2-syllable words: ph phonics phantom	No theme, story writing	Newspapers, state news Why did the events happen?	See Chapter Eight
101	2-syllable words: wr wrinkle wrongly	No theme, story writing	Newspapers, sports story Where did the event take place?	See Chapter Eight

No.	2-syllable words	Writing focus	Reading/Media activity	Reference
102	2-syllable words: dge ledger badger	No theme, story writing	Catalogues, clothing advertisements How are the clothes used?	See Chapter Eight
103	2-syllable words: tch itching watchful	No theme, story writing	Newspapers, classified advertisements: miscellaneous When should the seller be called by telephone?	See Chapter Eight
104	2-syllable words: nd ending bandage	No theme, story writing	Newspapers, news story of local interest Who is in the story?	See Chapter Eight
105	2-syllable words: ing ringlet raining	No theme, story writing	Newspapers, information about television programs Why are certain television programs shown?	See Chapter Eight
106	2-syllable words: ng unsung jingle	No theme, story writing	Catalogues, appliance advertisements What appliances are for sale?	See Chapter Eight
107	2-syllable words: ck rocket stacking	No theme, story writing	Newspapers, front page news story Where did the story take place?	See Chapter Eight
108	2-syllable words: cl cluster uncle	No theme, story writing	Newspapers, news story of local interest How is the story interesting?	See Chapter Eight
109	2-syllable words: er simmer certain	No theme, story writing	Newspapers, classified advertisements: pets What is the most expensive pet for sale?	See Chapter Eight
110	2-syllable words: or orchid anchor	No theme, story writing	Catalogues, toy advertisements When would the toys be used?	See Chapter Eight
111	2-syllable words: ar artful bargain	No theme, story writing	Newspapers, information about television programs Who are the leading characters?	See Chapter Eight
112	2-syllable words: oo toothless tatoo	Writing friendly letter	Magazines, reading a story Why is the story in the magazine?	See Chapter Eight
113	2-syllable words: ble scramble blender	Writing friendly letter	Magazines, reading a story What is the story about?	See Chapter Eight

LESSON	PHONICS/STRUCTURAL ANALYSIS	LANGUAGE EXPERIENCE	ACADEMIC, CULTURAL ARTS AND CURRENT EVENTS READING (Materials, Content Emphasis, and Guide for Comprehension)	RECREATIONAL READING
114	2-syllable words: al always signal	Writing memos	Telephone books, yellow pages: groceries Where are the grocery store listings?	See Chapter Eight
115	2-syllable words: ow shower showing	Writing memos	Magazines, reading advertisements How are the advertisements worded to sell the product?	See Chapter Eight
116	2-syllable words: ly early only	Writing story	Magazines, reading a story When did the story take place?	See Chapter Eight
117	2-syllable words: ll balloon windmill	Writing story	Magazines, reading advertisements Who is in the advertisements?	See Chapter Eight
118	2-syllable words: ed ended edit	Business letter	Magazines, completing forms Why is the form necessary?	See Chapter Eight
119	2-syllable words: un undo hundred	Business letter	Telephone books, yellow pages: automobiles What kinds of automobiles are for sale?	See Chapter Eight
120	2-syllable words: tr trusty trapper	Writing story	Magazines, reading a story Where did the story take place?	See Chapter Eight
121	2-syllable words: fl flashing flavor	Writing story	Magazines, reading a story How did one event happen in the story?	See Chapter Eight
122	3-syllable words: b probable bakery	Writing friendly letter	Magazines, reading a story Who is in the story?	See Chapter Eight
123	3-syllable words: c commonplace cereal	Writing friendly letter	Telephone books, yellow pages: appliances When would the appliance be used?	See Chapter Eight
124	3-syllable words: d divided dangerous	Writing story	Magazines, reading advertisements Why would the items be needed?	See Chapter Eight
125	3-syllable words: f following beautiful	Writing story	Magazines, reading advertisements What are items for children and items for adults?	See Chapter Eight

126	3-syllable words: g gallery argument	Writing business letter	Magazines, reading a story Where is a description of something in the story?	See Chapter Eight
127	3-syllable words: h hospital unhappy	Writing business letter	Telephone books, white pages: how to locate numbers How do you find numbers of persons named Smith, Jones and Brown?	See Chapter Eight
128	3-syllable words: j jellybean injury	Writing story	Magazines, reading a story When did one event in the story take place?	See Chapter Eight
129	3-syllable words: k kangaroo unlikely	Writing story	Magazines, reading advertisements Who is the advertiser?	See Chapter Eight
130	3-syllable words: l lemonade unlively	Writing story	Telephone books, white pages: how to locate numbers Why is Barnes before Block?	See Chapter Eight
131	3-syllable words: m mentioning armory	Writing list of items	Magazines, reading advertisements What items can be used in a living room?	See Chapter Eight
132	3-syllable words: n unity notable	Writing list of items	Magazines, reading a story Where are the characters from?	See Chapter Eight
133	3-syllable words: o obstacle origin	Writing story	Science textbooks, reading for main ideas How did something happen?	See Chapter Eight
134	3-syllable words: p, q popular important questioning aquatic	Writing story	Science textbooks, locating direction words When does something happen?	See Chapter Eight
135	3-syllable words: r recover remember	Writing poem	Social studies textbook, reading for main ideas Who is a part of the book?	See Chapter Eight
136	3-syllable words: s satisfy shimmering	Writing poem	Map reading, streets Why are streets shown on maps?	See Chapter Eight

LESSON	PHONICS/STRUCTURAL ANALYSIS	LANGUAGE EXPERIENCE	ACADEMIC, CULTURAL ARTS AND CURRENT EVENTS READING (Materials, Content Emphasis, and Guide for Comprehension)	RECREATIONAL READING
137	3-syllable words: t tomato tambourine	Writing poem	Social studies textbook, locating direction words What are some words indicating directions?	See Chapter Eight
138	3-syllable words: u unstable unify	Writing story	Mathematics textbook, locating direction words Where in problems are direction words?	See Chapter Eight
139	3-syllable words: v, w viable universe wonderful ownership	Writing story	Mathematics textbook, locating details in problems How does a detail describe something?	See Chapter Eight
140	3-syllable words: x, y, z xylophone taxation yodeling nursery zodiac zestfully	Writing story	Map reading, landmarks What route would be followed to visit a landmark?	See Chapter Eight
141	3-syllable words: a animal area	Writing poem	Science textbook, using context clues What are some context clues?	See Chapter Eight
142	3-syllable words: e enemy energy	Writing poem	Science textbook, locating descriptive words Who is described?	See Chapter Eight
143	3-syllable words: i idea irritate	Writing poem	Social studies textbook, using context clues Why are context clues helpful?	See Chapter Eight
144	3-syllable words: b balcony bionic	Writing story	Map reading, rivers What rivers are on the map?	See Chapter Eight
145	3-syllable words: c curious antarctic	Writing story	Social studies textbook, locating descriptive words Where are some descriptive words?	See Chapter Eight

178

No.	Words	Activity	Reading/Subject	Reference
146	3-syllable words: d / dynamic / recorded	Writing poem	Mathematics textbook, locating important facts / How are facts important?	See Chapter Eight
147	3-syllable words: e / elephant / element	Writing poem	Map reading, streets / What are the names of some of the streets or roads?	See Chapter Eight
148	3-syllable words: f / alfalfa / furniture	Writing poem	Mathematics textbook, locating descriptive words / Why is someone or something described?	See Chapter Eight
149	3-syllable words: g / generate / gingerly	Writing story	Science textbook, locating important facts / What are two important facts?	See Chapter Eight
150	3-syllable words: h / holiday / helplessness	Writing story	Science textbook, reading to draw conclusions / Where is a conclusion?	See Chapter Eight
151	3-syllable words: i / idiot / improper	Writing story	Social studies textbook, locating important facts / How do facts help?	See Chapter Eight
152	3-syllable words: j / jokingly / jeopardize	Writing poem	Map reading, landmarks / What are some landmarks?	See Chapter Eight
153	4 syllable words: k / kindergarten / kilometer	Writing poem	Mathematics textbook, specialized vocabulary / What are some mathematical words?	See Chapter Eight
154	4-syllable words: l / lamentable / alimony	Writing story	Newspapers, news story / When did the story take place?	See Chapter Eight
155	4-syllable words: m / municipal / monopoly	Writing story	Magazines, reading a story / Who is in the story?	See Chapter Eight
156	4-syllable words: n / harmonica / nonmetallic	Writing factual information	Completing forms / What important information is needed on the form?	See Chapter Eight
157	4-syllable words: o / overseer / oratory	Writing factual information	Catalogues, making a mock order / How do you complete the form?	See Chapter Eight

LESSON	PHONICS/STRUCTURAL ANALYSIS	LANGUAGE EXPERIENCE	ACADEMIC, CULTURAL ARTS AND CURRENT EVENTS READING (Materials, Content Emphasis, and Guide for Comprehension)	RECREATIONAL READING
158	4-syllable words: p, q apathetic pioneering aquarium questionable	Writing story	Telephone books, locating numbers What important numbers are in the front of the book?	See Chapter Eight
159	4-syllable words: r requisition radiantly	Writing story	Map, highways Where are four highways?	See Chapter Eight
160	4-syllable words: s security spectacular	Writing factual information	Completing forms Why is the form used?	See Chapter Eight
161	4-syllable words: t television traditional	Writing factual information	Science textbook, locating causes and effects What caused an effect?	See Chapter Eight
162	4-syllable words: u utility understanding	Writing factual information	Social studies textbook, locating causes and effects Where did the cause or effect take place?	See Chapter Eight
163	4-syllable words: v, w volleyball diversify weatherbeaten bewilderment	Writing story	Mathematics textbook, following directions How should the directions be followed?	See Chapter Eight
164	4 syllable words: x, y, z antitoxin auxiliary systematic hyperactive energizing enzymatic	Writing story	Newspapers, national news Who is in the news?	See Chapter Eight
165	4-syllable words: b boisterously benefited	Writing story	Completing forms Who should complete the form?	See Chapter Eight
166	4-syllable words: c continuous constructively	Writing factual information	Magazines, table of contents What is the main idea of different items in the table of contents?	See Chapter Eight

167	4-syllable words: d diplomatic radiator	Writing factual information	Catalogues, index Where are three different index items located?	See Chapter Eight
168	4-syllable words: f forgetfulness unfortunate	Writing story	Telephone books, yellow pages: schools What are the numbers of three schools?	See Chapter Eight
169	5-syllable words: g, h regurgitation sociology homogenizing oceanographer	Writing story	Completing forms Where should important information be placed on the form?	See Chapter Eight
170	5-syllable words: j, k juxtaposition joviality kaleidoscopic kleptomaniac	Writing story	Maps, planning a trip What route would be followed?	See Chapter Eight
171	5-syllable words: l, m liability nationality mathematical memorization	Writing factual information	Science textbooks, specialized vocabulary Where are some science words?	See Chapter Eight
172	5-syllable words: n, p nullification naturalistic pandemonium representative	Writing factual information	Social studies textbook, specialized vocabulary What are some social studies words?	See Chapter Eight
173	5-syllable words: q, r qualification quotability refrigerator radioactive	Writing story	Completing forms What directions are on the form?	See Chapter Eight
174	5-syllable words: s, t association solicitation transfiguration mystification	Writing story	Newspapers, news story How might the facts in the story affect someone?	See Chapter Eight

appendix five
Checklist for Teachers

Teachers should use this checklist at the end of the first month of teaching. Each item should be underway by the end of the first month or should be started as soon as possible during the second month of instruction.

ACADEMIC, CULTURAL ARTS, AND CURRENT EVENTS READING MODULES

____ 1. Use a variety of books related to the content area.

____ 2. Don't skip the Academic, Cultural Arts, and Current Events Reading Modules; they should begin to be easier to teach as students develop the concept of looking in print for specific information.

CHARTS

____ 3. Hang word, word clusters, and sentence charts around the classroom so each chart can be read.

____ 4. If necessary, string lines across classroom for display of charts. Use front and back of charts hung on lines.

____ 5. Include clusters, syllabication, etc., in words selected from students for charts. Emphasis should move beyond single syllable words to reflect clusters containing at least one multisyllable word.

____ 6. Occasionally use charts for review purposes.

GROUPING

____ 7. Work with individuals at their desks rather than placing students into traditional small reading-ability groups for instruction.

LANGUAGE EXPERIENCE MODULES

___ 8. Write some of the key words from Language Experience lead-in discussion on chart paper or on chalkboard before students begin their writing. Students may want to use some of these words in their stories but should not be required to do so.

___ 9. Call attention to at least one proofreading emphasis in each Language Experience Module.

MATERIALS

___ 10. Send books home at least three times a week. Send a book home as soon as a student can read one word in it. Consider basal readers as books of short stories.

___ 11. Consider requesting use of funds to purchase newspaper, magazine, and comic book subscriptions for delivery to the classroom.

___ 12. Use newspapers in the classroom.

___ 13. Use magazines in the classroom.

___ 14. Use science, social studies, and mathematics textbooks in the classroom.

___ 15. Encourage students to use dictionaries when needed and especially during the Language Experience Modules. Use dictionary to set a model for students.

___ 16. Use encyclopedias as soon as (and if) they become available. Begin showing one or two students at a time how to look up some item in the encyclopedia. By the end of the year, students should know how to use an encyclopedia.

OBJECTIVES

___ 17. Recognize the possibility that first graders can learn to read from a variety of printed materials, to write independently, and to enjoy both.

___ 18. Include comprehensive questions as a direct outgrowth of information that results in a module.

___ 19. Encourage students to *think* in each module.

___ 20. Use professional initiative in developing the program.

___ 21. Do not attempt to follow all lesson directions in the teacher's edition of a commercial program along with this program.

___ 22. Avoid having students memorize words, including lists of "sight" words.

___ 23. Have writing instruction in conjunction with reading lessons.

PARENTS

___ 24. Inform parents of a general overview of the program.

___ 25. Encourage parents and other interested persons to visit the classroom.

___ 26. Encourage parents to volunteer to help the teacher and students in the classroom.

PATTERNING MODULES

___ 27. Don't skip Patterning Modules; they are both remedial and enrichment (depending on the vocabulary selected) aspects of the program.

___ 28. Use a variety of reinforcement activities after the words are selected for use in the Patterning Modules.

PHONICS/SPELLING MODULE

_____ 29. Move from study of individual words to study of word clusters and to sentences.

_____ 30. Use vocabulary suggested by students and teachers in the classroom rather than relying exclusively on words in print.

_____ 31. Help students "sound-out" or decode unknown words as they are encountered in various kinds of printed materials.

_____ 32. Work with individual students for review of phonic skills during the writing parts of the Phonics/Spelling Modules.

RECORDS

_____ 33. Use a cardboard box for student papers from _each_ of (1) Phonics/Spelling; (2) Language Experience; and (3) Academic, Cultural Arts, and Current Events Reading Modules.

_____ 34. File a folder for each student in each box.

_____ 35. Have students file their papers in boxes _each day_. Students who can should do their own filing.

_____ 36. Date each paper before it is filed. Do not send these papers home until the end of the year.

_____ 37. Make a stencil copy _for each student_ of the form in Chapter Seven. Students should be encouraged to complete this form as a part of the Recreational Reading Modules.

_____ 38. Keep the principal informed of the progress of the students in the program.

RECREATIONAL READING MODULES

_____ 39. Keep library books in the classroom and establish a rotation system of exchanging books.

_____ 40. Emphasize quiet during the Recreational Reading Modules except for the individual conferences between teacher and one student.

_____ 41. Use guide in Recreational Reading Module lessons during conferences. Don't skip these conferences. They are one of the built-in remedial aspects in this program.

_____ 42. Exchange library books frequently to bring different books to the class.

SCHEDULING

_____ 43. Post a schedule of the times each module is taught outside the classroom door.

_____ 44. Keep the internal module components in each lesson moving at a pace that will prevent students from becoming bored while waiting for the next set of directions.

_____ 45. Teach all modules within each lesson.

_____ 46. Observe the time and avoid extending some lessons at the expense of others.

_____ 47. Ask a volunteer to sit beside a student who needs extra help in completing parts of the module lesson underway.

Results of Pre- and Poststandardized Tests

The reading section of the California Achievement Test,[1] Form A, Level 1, was administered in October 1976, as a pretest to all first graders in the Durham City Schools. Form B, Level 1 of the CAT was administered to all first graders as a posttest in May 1977. Two teachers were present during the administration and scoring of the tests.

Tables 9–11 show the reported test results. Although the results favor the experimental program (*Success in Beginning Reading and Writing*) over the control program (the Holt series was the lead basal),[2] any conclusion based on the test information must be taken cautiously. Among the limitations that should be observed are:

1. The experimental program did not begin until mid-October. Thus, this group did not receive the benefit of a full school year's exposure to the experimental program.

2. Experimental and control classes were in the same schools, and it was impossible to prevent control teachers from using parts of the experimental program, and vice versa. For example, charts similar to those in the experimental classes appeared in some control classes, and there was a noticeable increase over past years in the writing of language experience stories in some of the control classes.

3. The following data represent only a six-month trial of the experimental program.

4. Standardized test scores do not indicate motivation, self-concept about reading, and interest in reading.

Table 9 shows that the experimental group achieved a mean score of approximately five months beyond that of the control group. On the pretest, the means of the control and experimental groups were each 0.6; however, any total raw score between 0 and 58 gives a grade equivalent of 0.6 on the *California Achievement Test*. On the posttest, the control group's mean score was equal to expected grade level, whereas the experimental group was above grade level.

Table 10 shows the number and percent of control and experimental students who scored in each of

---

[1]Ernest W. Tiegs and Willis W. Clark. *California Achievement Tests.* Monterey, Calif.: CTB/McGraw-Hill, 1971.

[2]Eldonna L. Evertts et al. *The Holt Basic Reading System.* New York: Holt, Rinehart and Winston, Inc., 1973.

TABLE 9   Comparison of Pre- and Posttests—Grade Equivalents

SCHOOL	GRADE EQUIVALENT SCORES PRETEST		GRADE EQUIVALENT SCORES POSTTEST		DIFFERENCE	
	Control	Experimental	Control	Experimental	Control	Experimental
A	.6	.6	1.45	1.80	.85	1.20
B	.6	.6	1.96	2.92	1.36	2.32
C	.6	.6	1.69	1.85	1.09	1.25
D	.6	.6	2.76	2.58	2.16	1.98
E	no controls	.6	—	2.13	—	1.53
F	1.1	.6	3.50	3.43	2.40	2.83
G	.6	.8	2.07	2.27	1.47	1.47
Mean	.6	.6	1.97	2.52	1.37	1.92

Control Classes = 13
Experimental Classes = 17

TABLE 10   Comparison of Students—Posttest

GRADE EQUIVALENT SCORES	NUMBER OF STUDENTS		PERCENTAGE OF STUDENTS	
	Control	Experimental	Control	Experimental
5.0 and above	2	15	.6	3.6
4.0—4.9	12	32	3.8	7.7
3.0—3.9	26	62	8.3	15.0
2.0—2.9	115	178	36.9	43.2
1.0—1.9	97	91	31.1	22.0
below 1.0	59	34	18.9	8.2
			99.6	99.7

Control, N = 311
Experimental, N = 412

several intervals according to grade placement on the posttest; 80.4 percent of the control group scored a grade equivalent of 1.0 or above compared to 91.5 percent of the experimental group; and 43 percent of the control group scored 2.0 and above compared to 69.7 percent of the experimental group. Of the control group, 12.4 percent scored 3.0 and above compared with 27.0 percent of the experimental group, and 4.4 percent of the control group scored 4.0 and above compared to 11.2 percent of the experimental group. Less than 1 percent (0.6 percent) of the control group scored 5.0 and above compared to 3.6 percent of the experimental group. In general, a larger percentage of students in the experimental group achieved grade equivalent scores of 1.0 or better than did control group students. A smaller percentage of experimental group students scored lower than 1.0 than did control group students.

Table 11 shows that 34 percent of the control group students scored in the 80th percentile and above compared to 59 percent of the experimental students. At the lower extremes, 26 percent of the control students scored below the 40th percentile compared to only 12 percent of the experimental students.

186

TABLE 11   National Percentiles—Posttest

PERCENTILE	NUMBER OF STUDENTS		PERCENTAGE OF STUDENTS	
	Control	Experimental	Control	Experimental
90–99	74	179	23.8	43.4
80–89	34	67	10.9	16.3
70–79	34	34	10.9	8.2
60–69	35	28	11.3	6.8
50–59	27	31	8.7	7.5
40–49	24	23	7.7	5.6
30–39	19	15	6.1	3.6
20–29	29	22	9.3	5.3
10–19	23	10	7.4	2.4
0–19	12	3	3.8	.7

Control, $N = 311$
Experimental, $N = 412$

Teacher Opinions of the Success in Beginning Reading and Writing Program

The following are transcriptions from audio tape interviews made on March 8, 1977, with four teachers who taught the *Success in Beginning Reading and Writing* program for the first time in 1976–77. Their number of years of teaching experience ranges from one to twenty-six. Two of the teachers are black and two are white. Their comments are representative of the expressed opinions of the other teachers of the experimental classes.

The teachers were asked to describe the strengths and weaknesses in the program; the effect this program has had on how they teach reading; the effect of the program on above-average, average, and below-average students; the preference for an additional certified teacher or a teacher's aide to work with the students;[1] the comparison of this program with others taught in the past; and any other comments.

---

[1]This program had not been taught by a teacher and aide combination, and the effectiveness of that combination was unknown.

LINDA LEONARD
(9 years of teaching experience)

The biggest strength of this program is [that] it is designed to enable us to work individually with more children. The children have a lesson plan that they follow every day, and each child can work individually up to his or her capabilities. The various modules with a time framework are good because they help the children realize that they have a certain amount of work to do in a certain period, they concentrate on what they're doing, they know that they have to get it done because they will be moving to a different segment of the program. They have now [March 8, 1977] geared themselves to the 30-minute blocks and most of them do them successfully.

The main thing I would change right now is that one teacher should be able to work with another teacher all day long rather than only half a day. That way we could provide even more individual help during the rest of the day.

This program has changed the way I teach reading. I don't teach the regular three groups. I introduce the lesson to the whole class and then individually check students' work to see if they need individual help. I'm able to work with each student during

188

the 2½ hours several times, helping him or her become more creative and independent. This way, we help thirteen pupils each instead of twenty-six children, because there are two teachers. The children do their stories or writing exercises, and we have talking sessions with them. We get to know the children personally—what they like, what they don't like, things they do, things they like at school. In fact, they write stories about what we talk about and I read them, so I have gotten to know just about everything about the children with this program because their language experiences are so great.

The above-average child progresses very, very fast. In this program the children use dictionaries, and when the child gets through with his work (the above-average child is going to finish very quickly), there are different activities in the room for this child to do. This way, he or she is doing independent work on any level or topic the child wants to tackle.

The average child is progressing above grade level. It usually takes that student about 30 minutes to do what's required and for the teacher to check that child and listen to him or her read. If he or she finishes ahead of schedule, there are other activities to select from.

With below average children, we spend time helping them to finish what they are doing, and we start with what they can put on their papers. I have seen a definite improvement with the slower students. They are more creative and more enthusiastic. Often when they learn something, I hear, "Please let me read this to you."

In comparing the differences in working with another certified teacher and an aide, the job of the aide most of the time is to aid and assist the teacher in activities to be done. Aides do not take over the class teaching. They work with table work, make bulletin boards, and check papers. The aides do anything you ask them to, but as far as teaching the class, they do not do so. That is the job of the teacher.

This program is different from other programs I have taught. In this program, the child is able to go into depth in more aspects of the language arts and is able to do phonics, language, reading in different books at his or her own speed. The students get English, writing, and reading. This program really carries over into science, social studies, and other areas.

If other first grade teachers are interested in this program, I would encourage them to try it. I would like to see it in all the first grades in Durham or any other school system. If teachers have any questions, they should observe a couple of days to see how the children react to it and see how enthused and interested they are. They enjoy this program, and it's rewarding to see how well they have done.

This is a fantastic program. I enjoy working in it and think every first grade ought to have it if there is any way possible. I would really like to see a second teacher work in a first-grade classroom all day long teaching this program and helping in mathematics and other areas. I've enjoyed the program and have seen students progress more this year than any other year I previously taught.

MARY CHILDERS
(26 years of teaching experience)

One of the strengths of this program is moving from one module to another. I have seen children progress very rapidly and have a lot of time to do many things. They're very active in doing a variety of things, and we have a variety of things, and we have a variety of materials with which to work. We used to have a large number of children who couldn't read, but there isn't a child in this room who cannot read. The newspaper has been a great help. I only wish a child could have a newspaper to take home and read each day—they enjoy it. We enjoy working with it.

One thing I would like to change would be to have more time. There are some things that take more time, such as writing stories, and we have to stretch the module a little longer for some children. There are some children who need more help making up their stories than others. I've taught twenty plus years, and I can say this program has changed my ideas about children who can't learn to read. They *can* learn, and that's the way I feel about it. The children aren't afraid to read aloud; everybody in the room is ready to read. They might not know every word, but they have the courage to try to read, and we haven't had that before.

I have seen the above-average students move at a faster pace. We can provide for those children.

The average students are ahead. For example, they read more things, such as the Sears catalogue, and we talk about buying a pair of shoes. I don't tell them where to look for the shoes—they know how to pick up the catalogue, thumb through it until they find them, and then they know that there are shoes for $5.95 in the catalogue. Therefore, you bring in their mathematics from everyday living. This helps when they go to the store to purchase shoes.

The below-average children are moving forward. I have two children who were recommended for a special education class, but the children came to me instead, and they are actually reading now. They may not be as fast as some of the other children in the room, but they are reading.

I've worked with aides and with another teacher. Working with a teacher has been very helpful because the teacher has had experience, too, and knows how to work with children. Sometimes aides do not know how to work with children. It's a great help to discuss things—so it's great to work with another teacher.

In comparing this program to others I've taught, we use a variety of materials in this program and don't spend a lot of time with basals. The children go to the book shelves and pick any book they wish. If they need help, we will help, but we try to let them read the book first. If they have any problems, we're there to help them, but they can select any book to read. I would like to see this program continue because I believe the children would progress better with this type of instruction than the old way, and the children will feel as if they are learning something, which they are. They are at ease with their reading; they're not pressured and they know if they do not know something, we're there to help. Most of the time they can get it on their own. When someone asks me about using this program, I say, "Great, great, try it, you'll like it!"

ROXIE STEWART
(25 years of teaching experience)

This program is structured so that all of the children are challenged. They experience success, thereby creating a positive self-image. I also feel that a vocabulary built around their experiences is a strong motivational force when it comes to reading and writing stories.

The 30-minute modules must be flexible, and the 30 minutes used as a guide only. It is frustrating for children to be stopped in the middle of an activity when interest is very high and abruptly go into something else.

In this program, it is possible to do more individualized instruction with the children and the group-reading concept has been abolished. Those are some of the ways my teaching methods have changed.

The main difference between this program and others I've taught is found in the structure of this one—the way it's timed and its content flexibility. For example, every morning we get the newspapers, go through them, and talk about some of the articles. You see, I know some of the interests of the children. I usually discuss or read something to them, then stop when the interest level is very high. This morning, I talked about the helicopter that landed over on Hillside High School's campus. The children know and are interested in Hillside. I noticed when they had spare time, they went to get that newspaper to find out more. I didn't read and tell them all about it, just enough to create an interest in them. I like to do that every morning. Sometimes I get some magazines and talk about articles in them. I put the magazines down, and the next thing you know, they're getting those magazines to find out what I was talking about. I do that with the library books, also. I'll start reading a story sometimes, then say, "Oh, we don't have time to finish this, but it's in this book." I'll put the book down and next thing you know, someone will go and get that book. In fact, they'll go racing for that book. Stirring up interest and knowing what they are interested in is very important.

This program is constructed so that all of the children—above-average, average, and below-average—are able to work up to their potential. Additional challenges are available to them. There is more opportunity for individual contact with all of the children. They realize that they are important and that others are interested in their achievement. Children usually try to do what is expected of them if there is a feeling of love and warmth in the classroom.

When working with aides, success depends on how compatible you are. In working with a teacher, I notice that we usually complement each other. It seems as if we can understand problems and reach solutions in similar ways.

190

I've enjoyed working with this program, and I can see progress in the children. If a teacher asked me should he or she teach it, I would say teach it if you are interested in it. In any program, if someone doesn't want to do it, it's going to be a failure. But as for me, and where children are concerned, I'm for anything that will help them. If I can see children making progress, children learning, then I'm all for it. If you love children and are interested in their progress, this program is for you. If not, leave it alone because failure results from mediocrity.

A lot of satisfaction is derived while evaluating each day's activities. No other program I know about, even with two teachers, will accomplish what this one does for children.

MARCIA PAINTER
(1 year of teaching experience)

This reading program has many strong points. First of all, its structure allows all of the children in a classroom to discover and respond together. No child feels left out of what is happening, as is the possibility in a grouping situation. Next, the program is geared toward meeting the individual needs of each child, from the slowest to those who are average and above. Each child is challenged according to his or her own needs and abilities. He or she is able to readily identify with the vocabulary because it evolves from his own experience. No word is labeled too difficult to learn. Still another attribute of the program is its underlying emphasis upon the development of a positive self-concept within the child. Every child is given praise and encouragement, again, according to that which is considered a real accomplishment for that pupil, whether it be the ability to write his or her name correctly, or a detailed creative story. This taste of success provides the necessary incentive for the child to accept even greater challenges with confidence. Also, another positive aspect of the program lies in the emphasis it places upon the building of a strong phonics foundation. This foundation guides the children in the development of an ability to tackle new words with independence and ease. This will undoubtedly prove to be an invaluable tool to each child as he or she progresses beyond the first grade. Finally, and perhaps most important of all, this program does

much to guide the child in his or her own self-discovery of the joy and excitement found in reading. The active enthusiasm of the children is tremendous. Many times, when a child is asked if he or she would like to engage in a particular activity, the response will be . . . "I'd rather read a book." This testimony speaks for itself, and such an attribute toward reading will undoubtedly affect the child's performance in other areas of the curriculum in a very positive way. An immediate example of this effect has been observed in the area of mathematics. Children are able to solve simple word problems that many first graders would be unable to handle, because they can read and comprehend them.

My primary suggestion, as far as changes in the program are concerned, would be to establish a flexible time structure. This is especially applicable in the phonics module where *more* time than 30 minutes is a definite asset. If the children are stopped in the middle of an activity from which they are obviously benefiting in order to adhere to a strict time structure, they become a little frustrated. However, it is not recommended that the phonics module be extended at the expense of another module. Another minor alteration that might prove advantageous would be to insert the library book module midway into the 2½-hour block. This would allow it to serve as a change of pace—a departure from writing and verbalization to an atmosphere of relaxed reading for pleasure.

Since I am teaching this year for the first time, I can't speak from past years of experience in comparing this program with others. I am in total agreement with the program's attempt to stimulate the child's interest in reading and to provide experience in the areas of creative writing and reading for comprehension. The benefit of opening many new avenues of reading to the child at an early age has been clearly exhibited.

I would strongly recommend this program to other teachers. It does require a lot of work and commitment on the part of the teachers involved, but the results are well worth the time and effort. By having *two qualified* teachers working as a team, it is possible to individualize more with the children in meeting their specific needs. I would also recommend the program because it allows the children to become familiar with materials that they are going to encounter throughout their lives. They are not confined primarily to the basal reader, as is the case in many reading programs. In addition to this, they are exposed to the daily newspaper, magazines, textbooks, catalogues, and telephone directories—media that it will be necessary for them to cope with in the future.

This program allows each teacher to work more frequently on a one-to-one basis with all children. Therefore, insight is gained into each child's way of perceiving and learning. The teacher comes to better understand the personality of the student and can more readily recognize and answer to his or her individual needs.

This program definitely has helped me as a new teacher. It has the structure that is needed to accomplish the goals that are stated in its purpose; however, it is not without a degree of necessary flexibility. Each teacher is able to exercise his or her own professional judgment as to how a particular concept or activity will be taught. The basic outlines provided for each lesson are indicative of expert planning, and they do an excellent job of providing the classroom teachers with a launching point. They also serve to ensure that the necessary elements of the program are taught.

Again, this program does not confine the children to the basal reader and a limited number of supplementary books or workbooks. They are able to branch off into new fields of reading and self expression. This is the key to the stimulation of interest, while encounter with success serves as the key to motivation. The children in this program are genuinely enthused about reading, and this enthusiasm will undoubtedly affect their future years of education. Without a strong basic foundation in reading, a child will find it progressively difficult to reach his or her full potential in life. This innovative reading program does much to contribute to that foundation.

Index